ASKING SMART QUESTIONS

Jacqueline Frischknecht, Ph.D.
and
EllaMarie Schroeder

© 2006 Pieces of Learning
CLC0391
ISBN 1-931334-83-8
Cover Design John Steele

All rights reserved. In our effort to produce high quality educational products we offer portions of this book as "reproducible." Permission is granted, therefore, to the buyer - one teacher - to reproduce student activity pages in LIMITED quantities for students in the buyer's classroom only. The right to reproduce is not extended to other teachers, entire schools, or to school systems. Use of any pages on the Internet is strictly forbidden. No other part of this publication may be reproduced in whole or part. The whole publication may not be stored in a retrieval system, or transmitted in any form or by any means, electronic, mechanical, photocopying, recording, or otherwise without written permission of the publisher. For any other use contact Pieces of Learning at 1-800-729-5137. For a complete catalog of products contact Pieces of Learning or visit our Web Site at www.piecesoflearning.com

Asking Smart Questions

ACKNOWLEDGEMENTS

We wish to acknowledge our many students without whose suggestions this book would never have been written.

We are also indebted to the many researchers in the fields of question asking, accelerated learning, and multiple intelligences upon whose work this work is based.

A thank you is owed to Ward Flynn who suggested black hole questions and to Glenn Capelli whose work we often reference.

TABLE OF CONTENTS

An Invitation..5

Teaching Question-Asking Skills 10

HOME PAGE: From IQ To Iq (I Question)..............................12
INFO SITES
About Questions 16
The Need For Skills 20
The Question-Asking Process 28
Question Attributes 30
Word Choice 39
Question-Asking Alternatives 46

HOME PAGE: QUESTION TYPES 51
INFO SITES
The Basic Six — Plus 55
Useful Questions 59
Non-Productive and X-Rated Questions 61

HOME PAGE: SURFING THROUGH THE TIME ZONES 64
INFO SITES
The *Before* Zone 66
The *Interface* Between Zones 69
The *During* Zone 77
The *After* Zone 82
The *Seldom-If-Ever* Zone 84

HOME PAGE: THE DICTIONARIES 86
INFO SITES
Useful Questions... 91
Non-Productive Questions 114
X-Rated Questions 122

HOME PAGE: THE OTHER SIDE OF QUESTION ASKING 126
INFO SITES
Listening In the Time Zones.. 128
Re-Phrasing Poor Questions 133

Write Your Own Useful Questions... 136

Bibliography 140
INDEX 141

Asking Smart Questions

AN INVITATION . . .

We invite you
to set aside any preconceived ideas,
open your mind and your heart,
put on your professional thinking cap,
and explore the many ways of

ASKING SMART QUESTIONS

To take the leaps?
A provocative question is the only way that I've found.
— Bandrowski, James F

A Familiar Chinese Story

A poor man asked a wise man to give him a fish because his family was starving. But the wise man refused. Instead he offered to teach the poor man to fish because then his family would be fed every day, not just one day.

PARADIGM SHIFT

What the wise man offered the poor man was a ***paradigm shift*** — a different way to view his problem. That's what this book offers: a paradigm shift in the way you view questions. If you learn what kinds of questions to ask or what kinds of questions you are being asked, then you have begun to develop a precision tool for learning that will . . .

▶ make your professional life easier, more productive, and more fun.
▶ enable you, in the long run, to save time.

If you explore the techniques in this book, you'll also enhance your personal relationships. You don't have to do it all at once — just take a deep breath and, as they say in Australia, *"Give it a go!"*

Asking Smart Questions

HOW TO USE THIS BOOK

You don't necessarily need to read this book from cover to cover in the order in which it was written. (Although, of course, you could — the benefit being you get full value for your time!) But if that's not the most efficient way for you to accomplish your goals, there are other options. The book is organized to be useful as a reference tool. You might want to —

  Read only the Home Pages.

Benefit: You get a quick, general idea of how to ask SMART questions.

  Read only the Info Sites.

Benefit: You get detailed information, one step at a time, to deal with a specific subject.

  Read only the 'Bugs' section of the Dictionaries.

Benefit: You can quickly identify and find solutions for question- asking problems.

  Read only the Dictionaries.

Benefit: You get definitions and general information about specific question types.

  Read only the HOT TIPS.

Benefit: You get *just the facts'* to help you know what to do NOW!

Mental Bungee Jump

Follow the directions and Mental Bungee Jump from section to section.

Benefit: You can easily find more details or in-depth explanations of the topic you're exploring, or find new, related topics.

Mental Bungee Jumping?

You've heard of bungee jumping; it's a great way to plunge into the unknown. You can leap off tall buildings while remaining safely anchored to your own reality (even if you do wind up hanging by a proverbial thread . . !)

Mental bungee jumping is a terrific way to take an intellectual plunge . . . Go ahead, try it!

Mental Bungee Jumping is as simple as One-Two-Three.

HOW TO DO IT

▶ Start, for example, with the Table of Contents. Look at the section titled *Home Page, Question Types.* It includes sections on *The Basic Six — Plus, Useful Questions,* and *Non-Productive and X-Rated Questions.*

▶ Want to learn more about a specific Question Type without reading the entire section? First —

Mental Bungee Jump
To
Home Page:
Question Types
Page 51

Asking Smart Questions

There you'll find several other **Mental Bungee Jump** suggestions — look for the

Mental Bungee Jump
To
Dictionary of X-Rated
Questions
Page 122

▶ Jump there and you'll find a list of X-Rated Questions to be avoided.

CONGRATULATIONS!

You have successfully made some

Mental Bungee Jumps!

To continue, visualize elastic bridges stretching between all the subjects of this book. Jump on a mental bridge, grab a mental bungee cord, and bounce! Bungee Jump to . . .
- an **INFORMATION SITE**
- a **QUESTIONNAIRE**
- a **DICTIONARY OF QUESTION TYPES**
- another **INFORMATION SITE**
-

— whatever will be most useful to you. By using the Table of Contents and the Index, you can return to your starting point quickly and easily. You can go forward, backward, sideways, jump around — whatever works for *YOU*. The bottom line is, however you choose to use it,

ASKING SMART QUESTIONS

will help you improve your question-asking skills.

It will help you think through both your questions and answers, so you can be a more effective communicator. In short, this book will help you improve your communication skills.

THE QUESTION
Jay Frankston

When I was a child and I had a question
I asked my parents "Why?"
And whatever their answer happened to be
I kept on asking "Why?"
And they thought me a nuisance
and they thought it a game
and they told me to go out and play.
And though I insisted till they scolded me well
My question was here to stay.

TEACHING QUESTION-ASKING SKILLS

WHOSE QUESTIONS?

Traditionally, teachers bombard students with questions, both oral and written. Students, however, do not reciprocate. Research indicates that over a school year, the norm in K-12 classrooms is one student-generated question per student per month. (Dillon, 1988) To fill the gaps, teachers are producing 84 questions for every two student- produced questions during any given K-12 classroom hour. (Various researchers) We then expect students to give back **THE** answers that we have already determined to be correct. The future academic success of most students, therefore, rests on their ability to reproduce answers, produced by others, to questions generated by others, thus 'proving' they are educated or trained.

Teachers will serve students better if they help *students* become proficient at question asking — a skill in which most of them are novices. Recall the story of the wise man who declared that giving a man a fish made him dependent on others forever, but teaching the man how to fish made him independent forever. It's a lesson to remember and honor.

BENEFITS OF FLIP-FLOPPING

The benefits of taking the time to encourage and teach your students to develop question-asking skills are many. Good questions create excitement in the learning process and help produce good answers by . . .

> ▶ **stimulating thinking on many levels.**
>> ▶ **exploring new ways of viewing old ideas.**
>>> ▶ **sharing existing attitudes, values or ideas.**
>>>> ▶ **stimulating group discussion.**

By teaching question-asking skills to your students you will **immediately** have a whole classroom full of hands flying ceiling-wards. Your students will be eager to answer your stimulating questions and to generate their own; you will be impressed by the incisiveness of your students' thinking; and they will go home and actually respond with something more intelligent than "*I dunno*" to their parents' queries about the day's activities. (Actually, it probably won't instantly happen that way 100% of the time . . . but your chances of success will skyrocket.)

But, just as you would not expect your students to do well on an exam before they had plenty of time to acquire the necessary knowledge, so you wouldn't expect them to be good question askers without acquiring the necessary skills.

EXAMINE YOUR OWN SKILLS

The most basic language strategy used by teachers is questioning. So let's begin with questions for you in your teacher role:

▶ **Are classroom questions different from other types of questions?**

▶ **Are different question types required for different subject areas?**

To answer the first question: no, classroom questions are in essence no different from other types. And second, probably yes, to some extent different types of questions may be better suited to specific subject areas.

In order to teach others how to ask good questions, you need to be confident that you are skilled in question asking.

HOW TO DO IT

▶ Cultivate a mind-set that recognizes and honors the wide variance in thinking styles.
▶ Model the kinds of questioning behavior you want your students to develop.
▶ Be clear about why you ask a particular question and what result you are seeking.
▶ Assess how well your questions work.
▶ Examine how you and your students can improve your skill sets.

As a teacher, you are no doubt already skilled at generating good questions. It is understood you have time limitations. But (and there is always a 'but') since limited time and attention in teacher education is devoted to learning question-asking skills, most educators can use help in developing and/or refining those skills.

HOT TIP

The payoff is spectacular!

If we are successful in helping students learn how to ask good questions, our students may actually become educated or trained (learn how to fish!) — *they will have learned how to learn!*

Asking Smart Questions

HOME PAGE

From IQ to Iq (I question)

*The first key to wisdom is this —
constant and frequent questioning . . .*
— Peter Abelard

The Iq Factor

You know about IQ tests: question after daunting question that you must answer to prove how smart you are. Let's think about a flip. Suppose that instead of answering questions to prove how smart you are, you had to *ask* questions to prove how smart you are. This is the premise of our Iq Factor — **I QUESTION**. Consider these opinions:

The important thing is not to stop questioning.
— Albert Einstein

We judge a man by his questions, rather than his answers.
— Voltaire

*How we ask and respond to questions
reveals our highest forms of intelligence.*
— Robert Sternberg

But is that how it happens in real life? Consider this amazing but true story told by Glenn Capelli:

Case in Point

Andrew Belotti, a wonderful Australian teacher, routinely teaches his Year 7 students how to ask questions and to love the questioning process. His methods have won him and his class many awards in the learning of science. One year, the Year 8 teachers conducted a survey of their new students. All of Andrew's former students tested high in the asking of questions. The information that was fed back to Andrew was —
"Mr. Belotti, your students ask too many questions. In the future, please teach in such a way as to limit this practice."

QUESTIONS FOR YOU

- Is question asking a skill which can be learned?
- Is question asking a skill people need to learn?

We believe the answer to both questions is "Yes." However, as Tony Stockwell, an educator in Liechtenstein, reminds us:

> It's not what you do,
> it's the way that you do it,
> that's what gets results!

This is very true of the **Iq** FACTOR. Anyone can ask questions, but our *question smartness* comes with the *way we ask* the questions.

Asking questions *seems* to be the most simple and direct form of communication. But in reality, it can be a complicated process. There are two main steps to asking **SMART** questions. First, you must understand the question-asking process. Second, you must know what kind of question to ask and how to ask it (which necessarily includes knowing what kinds of questions are possible to ask). The whole point is to get useful, intelligent answers without having to resort to pulling teeth.

> **HOT TIP**
> The five W's (Who? What? When? Where? Why?) and the very important H's (How much? How many?) of question asking are essential factors in mastering the development of your own Iq.

Mental Bungee Jump
To
Info Site:
About Questions
Page 16

Asking Smart Questions

QUESTIONNAIRE: WHAT DO I KNOW?

The thing I am most aware of is my limits.
— Andre Gide

Directions Respond to the following statements by checking the box that most closely describes you. There are no right or wrong answers.

I KNOW . . .	Yes	Maybe	No
1. there are many different types of questions.			
2. the five basic "W" types of questions.			
3. the difference between useful questions and not-useful questions.			
4. at least fifteen different kinds of questions.			
5. the appropriate times to use specific question-types.			
6. that the way I ask a question can influence the type and quality of the answer I receive.			
7. how to ask questions so I can get the type of answer (fact/opinion, detailed/broad, etc.) I am looking for.			
8. how to avoid using words that can be interpreted in different ways when I ask a question.			
9. the difference between non-productive and hostile questions.			
10. the difference between an open and a closed question.			
I THINK OR BELIEVE THAT . . .	Yes	Maybe	No
11. asking questions comes naturally and is not a skill that needs to be developed.			
12. that asking good questions is an important skill I should develop further.			
13. that I can improve my question-asking ability.			

Asking Smart Questions

I UNDERSTAND . . .	Yes	Maybe	No
14. the role listening plays in the question-asking process.			
15. how the non-verbal aspect of asking a question can change the meaning of the question.			
16. the differences between leading and loaded questions.			
17. that questions can be asked to intimidate, to show off, or to play dumb.			
18. that the questions I ask can increase or decrease my credibility with others.			
19. that the assumptions which underlie questions affect the meaning of the question.			
20. that my tone of voice will influence the quality of the reply I receive.			
21. that it is important to pay attention to timing when asking questions.			
22. that if I'm clear about the message I intend to send by asking a question, I will be more likely to be understood.			
23. that question asking is a process, not an isolated incident.			
24. that the situation in which a question is asked can influence both the meaning of the question and the answer received.			
25. that a question is a powerful, multi-purpose communication tool.			

What have you learned? Use the **ASKING SMART QUESTIONS** book to learn more and improve any areas where you gave a 'MAYBE' or a 'NO' answer.

Asking Smart Questions

 **INFO SITE**

About Questions

*Once you have learned how to ask relevant and appropriate questions,
you have learned how to learn
and no one can keep you
from learning whatever you want or need to know."*
— Neil Postman

A question is a powerful *communication* tool. It can be used to push, pull, pry, stimulate, threaten, remind, reason, warn, tease, nag, clarify, influence (you could read 'manipulate'), build up, destroy, create — the list is endless. A question can send you on a flight of fancy or yank you back to reality. It can launch you on a journey into foreign territories — intellectually, emotionally, or even literally. And like any other powerful tool, a computer, for example, a question can make your life more difficult or considerably easier. The consequences of being clumsy in the use of a question are usually less than the consequences of a computer disaster or failure, but the principle is similar. (The same computer or question that, under normal circumstances, speeds and facilitates your projects — can, under different conditions, play the starring role in a real life comedy of errors.) You will get better results if you learn more about how to ask **SMART** questions (and give **SMART** answers).

> **HOT TIP**
> *Maybe some questions about questions would be in order!*

Questions about questions? Is that sensible? Kipling warned, *"Them that asks no questions isn't told a lie."* But Einstein insisted, *"The important thing is not to stop questioning."* And Voltaire recommended we *"Judge a man by his questions, rather than by his answers."*

But a question is a question is a question — right?

Absolutely not. Some questions are inherently better than others. Good questions are *designed* to get to the core information the questioner wants. Poor questions don't accomplish the job they set out to do.

Asking Smart Questions

Does it matter HOW you ask questions?

Only if you care about the quality of the answers you get. Crummy questions tend to produce crummy — or no — answers.

What about these questions, can you answer any of them?

▶ Why are questions so important?

▶ How can I tell which type of question would be most appropriate for a particular situation?

▶ Does it make any difference WHAT KINDS of question I ask?

▶ How can I tell a good question from a bad one?

▶ How can I tell a better question from a merely 'satisfactory' one?

▶ How do I know when I'm successful and when I'm not?

Need some answers? First:

Mental Bungee JUMP
To
Questionnaire:
What Do I Know
Page 14

You probably STILL have questions about questions. For example —

▶ How many different types of questions are there?

▶ How will knowing how to ask SMART questions help students learn faster and better — and improve their grades?

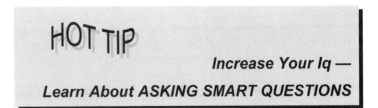
HOT TIP
Increase Your Iq —
Learn About ASKING SMART QUESTIONS

Asking Smart Questions

Use the Index to

Mental Bungee JUMP

All Around This Book
For The Information You Need

You might still be wondering . . .

Why are questions so important?

Questions are among the most powerful communication tools at our disposal. On a personal level, questions can be used to show interest and demonstrate caring; to display either knowledge or ignorance; or even to assert independence. They can be used for self-revelation and for seeking knowledge about others.

> **HOT TIP**
> *A well-phrased question can give the asker keys to other people — to HOW THEY THINK AND HOW THEY FEEL*

On an intellectual level, questions can focus the direction of your thoughts and unlock or transform your knowledge. For example, for centuries people asked, *"WHY does the ball fall?"* Galileo asked, *"HOW does the ball fall?"* That question lead Newton to consider, discover, and ultimately formulate his laws of physics. And that makes question asking (and the person who masters the skill) a power to be reckoned with!

> **HOT TIP**
> To make yourself and your questions
> a power to be reckoned with,
> choose the question most appropriate for the situation.

Asking Smart Questions

QUESTION CHOICE

*No; we have been as usual asking the wrong question.
It does not matter a hoot what the mockingbird
on the chimney is singing . . .
The real and proper question is: Why is it beautiful?*
— Annie Dillard

Another important question to ask about questions is:

Does it make any difference WHAT KINDS of question you ask?

And the answer is ***Yes, it makes a big difference***. Certainly all questions share common goals: to find out what you don't know, further your understanding or increase your empathy. However, questions vary considerably in PURPOSE and STYLE, so it's important to know which type to use when. You wouldn't use a screwdriver to drive in a nail if you had a hammer easily accessible, would you? Nor would you use a golf swing when you stepped up to bat. The same is true of questions. With the wide variety of types available, it's simply more efficient to use questions designed for specific purposes.

> **HOT TIP**
> *You can tailor your questions to meet your specific needs.*

**Mental Bungee JUMP
To
Home Page:
Question Types
page 51**

Asking Smart Questions

 INFO SITE

The Need for Skills

*I question things and do not find
One that will answer to my mind*
— William Wordsworth

Do you need question-asking skills?

Does it really matter if you know HOW to ask questions?

You wouldn't expect to operate a complicated power tool with no instruction in its use, would you? Yet few parents seriously feel their children need help learning to ask questions. Far from it! Every three-year-old asks questions, and by the time children are four or five, their beleaguered parents fervently wish they'd stop.

Case in Point

Kid: Mom, why do I have to have Sally for a baby-sitter?

Mom: Because she lives next door and she does a good job.

Kid: Why can't I have someone different?

Mom: Because it's hard to find a good sitter and she likes to come.

Kid: But Why do I have to have her?

Mom: Don't you like Sally?

Kid: Yes, but why can't I have someone else?

Mom: Because I can't find anyone else close by.

Kid: Why not?

Mom: Because no other baby-sitters live in our neighborhood.

Kid: Why Not?

Asking Smart Questions

? Pertinent Question ¿
Since even young children feel perfectly comfortable throwing questions about with reckless abandon, WHY would anyone need a book about questions and how to ask them?

Answer
Because the process doesn't always work as advertised!

You ask questions on a very regular basis in *all* of your life roles. In your professional life, as a family member or friend, you ask questions all day, every day. It's part of your job. And answering your questions is supposed to be the job of your listeners. So it should be easy. You, unlike the perpetual *why?*-asking child, ask well-thought-out, pertinent questions. You receive well-thought-out, pertinent answers. Right?

You know it doesn't always work that way. In fact, sometimes it gets so crazy you probably feel like you're suddenly speaking Latin in a room full of Norwegian immigrants on the Moon! At the very least, your English and your listeners' English seem to be different languages with very few commonalities. What happened?

In plain English, question asking and answering, like other communication skills, are natural processes. Unfortunately, we tend to take natural processes — especially those learned in childhood — for granted. In fact, their naturalness makes them transparent: we see right through the process, not even realizing it *is* a process. That means that most of us don't realize we could learn to do it better.

> **HOT TIP**
> *You will get better results
> (and make your life easier)
> if you learn more about how to use your tools —
> in this case, How To Ask Questions.*

Asking Smart Questions

QUESTION ASKERS

Are all questioners equal to their task?

Most definitely not. Some people (depending on cultural background as well as individual personality) feel that asking a lot of questions appears rude, presumptuous, or invasive. Some feel that asking questions makes them seem 'dumb'. Still others make a sincere effort to ask questions, but find it difficult to put into words exactly what it is they want to know. They stumble, falter, try first one arrangement of words, then another. And then, even when they get it right and the words send a clear message, other factors, such as the manner in which the question is asked, can influence the reply received.

And you thought question asking was a natural process at which even three-year-olds were proficient . . . It really does depend on how you define 'proficient', doesn't it?

> *If you are Question-asking-impaired or even just Question wary, your condition is not beyond repair.*
>
> **HOT TIP**

Asking questions is a universal activity for all people, in all languages. Asking **SMART** questions is a particular skill acquired by people with a passion to communicate effectively.

HOW TO DO IT

▶ Start at the very beginning . . .

▶ Find out what you already know about asking questions and how good you are, right now, at question asking.

Mental Bungee JUMP
To
Home Page:
Question Types
page 51

Asking Smart Questions

GOOD QUESTIONS — POOR QUESTIONS

Are all questions equal to their task?

Absolutely not. Some questions are inherently better than others. Good questions are *designed* to get to the core information the questioner wants. Poor questions don't accomplish the job they set out to do. Many poor questions suffer design and/or construction flaws. Some, like hostile *Gotcha* questions, for example, are so totally non-productive they serve more to shoot the asker in the foot than to elicit an answer.

It's hard to avoid a snake in the grass if your eye isn't trained to notice . . .
HOT TIP *Learn more about question flaws!*

But how can you tell a good question from a poor one?
and
How can you tell a better question from a merely 'satisfactory' one?

Start by listening to the answer you receive . . . good questions usually get reasonably good answers; poor ones usually don't. Sometimes it's hard to distinguish an answer you don't like from a 'bad' answer. So, since you have this book, you can take a more scientific approach. Investigate the dictionaries. They are full of good questions *and* problem questions. You'll also find suggestions on how to change problem questions into better ones.

Mental Bungee JUMP
To
The Dictionaries:
Useful Questions
Not-Useful Questions
X-Rated Questions
page 86

Asking Smart Questions

? Pertinent Question ¿

How do you know when you're successful and when you're not?

> **HOT TIP**
> *If you get a useful answer,*
> *and if you keep communication lines open,*
> *you probably asked a good question,*
> *and you're successful.*

But if you're worried about it, remember —

> **HOT TIP**
> *You can easily increase*
> *your question-asking*
> *and answering effectiveness.*

HOW TO DO IT

▶ Consciously pay attention to how you phrase your questions, how others might perceive your questions, and how essential it is to be accurate.

Asking Smart Questions

QUESTIONNAIRE: MY QUESTION-ASKING SKILLS

*Humility is not my forté,
and whenever I dwell for any length of time
on my own shortcomings,
they gradually begin to seem mild,
harmless, rather engaging little things,
not at all like the staring defects in other people's characters.*
— Margaret Halsey

DIRECTIONS: Do you know how you rate as a question-asker? Rate yourself on the following questions. There are no right or wrong, good or bad, answers.

	Usually	Sometimes	Seldom
1. I ask good questions.			
2. When I ask a question, I know what type of question it is.			
3. I give thought to phrasing my questions before I open my mouth to speak.			
4. I am aware of the non-verbal cues I'm sending when I ask questions.			
5. When I ask a question, I have in mind the kind of answer I would like to receive.			
6. When I meet someone new, the first thing I do is ask a lot of questions.			
7. I am careful to give people sufficient time to answer my question before I ask a second question.			
8. I'm careful to avoid sexist language when I ask questions.			
9. I'm careful to avoid jargon when I ask questions.			
10. When I'm not sure of myself or my information, I ask questions.			
11. When people ask me question after question, I become impatient and irritated.			

© 2006 Pieces of Learning

Asking Smart Questions

QUESTIONNAIRE: MY QUESTION-ASKING SKILLS

	Usually	Sometimes	Seldom
12. I give conscious thought to my choice of question-type before I ask a question.			
13. I understand the answers I receive and don't need to ask further questions.			
14. In a new situation, I tend to ask a lot of questions.			
15. My intention in asking a question is to get a true and accurate reply.			
16. I do well when I am being interviewed.			
17. I listen carefully to answers I receive.			
18. I feel confident that I ask questions that encourage people to feel comfortable answering me.			
19. My favorite type of question begins with "*Why.*"			
20. My favorite type of question begins with "*What.*"			
21. My favorite type of question begins with "*How.*"			
22. I like to ask for as much information as possible in one question.			
23. I approach life with a questioning attitude.			
24. I take care to phrase a question so it can be easily understood.			
25. When I ask a question I sincerely want an answer.			
26. When I ask questions I look directly at the person to whom I am speaking.			

Asking Smart Questions

QUESTIONNAIRE: MY QUESTION-ASKING SKILLS

	Usually	Sometimes	Seldom
27. I don't use questions to hide my uncertainty or ignorance.			
28. I am willing to re-phrase my questions if the other person doesn't understand.			
29. I don't use questions as put-downs, or to intimidate others or make others feel uncomfortable.			
30. I like to ask questions, because it helps me get to know someone better.			
31. I think asking a lot of questions makes me appear dumb.			
32. I tend to ask questions that will guide others toward my way of thinking.			
33. I am good at interviewing.			
34. I always ask myself questions about lots of different things.			
35. I think it is rude to ask a lot of questions.			
36. I often answer a question with a question.			
37. I use questions to deflect blame from myself.			

What do your answers tell you about your question-asking ability?

Asking Smart Questions

 **INFO SITE**

The Question-Asking Process

*The centipede was happy quite
Until a toad in fun
Said, "Pray, which leg goes after which?"
That worked her mind to such a pitch,
She lay distracted in a ditch,
Considering how to run.*
— Mrs. Edward Craster

WHY IS QUESTION-ASKING A PROCESS?

Consider what happens when you just open your mouth and let loose whatever happens to be there, on the tip of your tongue. Sometimes it works. But often you find yourself backtracking — **What I really meant was** . . . And you still get exactly the kind of insufficient answers such a haphazard approach deserves! You can't jump feet-first into question asking and expect to be successful. When you do, neither you nor your innocent, unsuspecting listener stands a chance of a quality information-exchange. You can avoid this sort of problem by learning about the question-asking process; it's sort of the A, B, Cs of question asking.

WHAT IS THE QUESTION-ASKING PROCESS?

The question-asking process actually begins before you open your mouth. The FIRST step involves thinking and planning. You will need to simultaneously handle all aspects of the communicative process, while negotiating the interfaces and transitions between question-asking time zones. Receiving an answer is the LAST step.

Asking Smart Questions

There are five basic steps in the question-asking process:

STEP 1: Determine the **type of question** you want to ask.

STEP 2: Consider the **attributes** of question asking.

STEP 3: Proceed to that **in-between place**.

STEP 4: Then: **ASK** the question, and get an **ANSWER**.

STEP 5: Consider the answer you receive so you will know if you need to **ask another question.**

Each step will be easier if you do some Mental Bungee Jumping —

Mental Bungee JUMP

To

Step 1: Home Page: Question Types - 51

**Step 2: Info Sites: The *Before* Zone - 66
Question Attributes - 30**

**Step 3: Info Site: The *Interface*
Between The Zones - 69**

Step 4: Info Site: The *During* Zone - 77

Step 5: Info Site: The After-Zone

HOT TIP *Don't panic. You don't have to mount a major campaign every time you want to ask a question! With a little practice, most of the process will become automatic.*

Asking Smart Questions

 **INFO SITE**

Question Attributes

The question is, said Alice,
whether you can make words mean so many different things.
— Lewis Carroll

Choosing a question-type is an important first step. The second step in the process is to consider the attributes of your question. You need to *deliberately think* about:

▶ Timing

  ▶ Situation

    ▶ Pacing

      ▶ Sequencing

        ▶ Assumptions

          ▶ Word Choices

Take a few moments to make a quick inventory of what you need to know.

HOW TO DO IT

▶ Scan through this section quickly, only stopping to read in detail what's new to you.

HOT TIP
*"Take a few moments"
might mean you take 5 minutes or 30 —
It depends on how much is new information
and how much is review.*

Asking Smart Questions

TIMING

Knowing WHEN and HOW OFTEN to ask questions is vital. Ask yourself:
- Is the current speaker finished and open to questions now?
- Is this question appropriate at this point in the conversation?
- Or might I get a better answer by waiting?

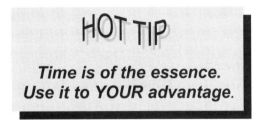

HOT TIP

Time is of the essence. Use it to YOUR advantage.

SITUATION

The context in which you ask a question has a direct influence on the type of question that will be most effective. Before asking your question, ask yourself:

How does this particular situation affect the question I want to ask?

How does the situation influence the way I ask my question?

For example: a vice-principal questioning a vandalism suspect will need to ask different types of questions than a classroom teacher:

Vice Principal: ***Where were you and who were you with Friday night?***

Teacher: ***What is the importance of the Fifth Amendment?***

Clearly, the situation plays a role in determining what type of question is appropriate.

HOT TIP

If you step all over a person's sensibilities by asking questions that are inconsistent with the situation, you are most likely to get non-answers, evasions, and defensiveness.

Asking Smart Questions

PACING

Pacing has to do with how rapidly or slowly you ask your questions. Consider this style:

Why are you late <u>Again</u>? Don't give me your usual so-called reasons; I want to know right now — what is your excuse this time? What could possibly have caused you to be late when you knew important it was to be here on time? Well? What have you got to say?

This is certainly not a calm, unhurried question-asking manner intended to give your listeners time to grasp your meaning and reply in a way that expresses their ideas or feelings. In the right situation — a lawyer engaged in cross-examination, attempting to 'encourage' a witness to disclose information she doesn't wish to give — such a rapid-fire, staccato pace might be appropriate. Otherwise, firing one question after another in a demanding, answer-me-now style is likely to be intimidating, and worse, guarantee poor quality answers from your now defensive answerers.

But courtroom lawyers aren't the only ones with a bad question-asking reputation. Many people find questions from a teacher just as intimidating as those from a prosecuting attorney. And it's not only because they're afraid they might not know the answer — they're concerned about the question-asker's style.

> **Research Report**
>
> In the case of students and teachers, the average lapse of time between a student's answer and the teacher's next question is LESS THAN ONE SECOND! (Rowe, 1974. No new research indicates that teachers have slowed down.) And on top of that, many teachers seem to have an almost irresistible urge to interrupt.

Who wouldn't be intimidated when they know they're expected to answer, but they can hardly manage to wedge their replies in between a teacher's questions and interruptions?

People tend to believe a hurried questioner has no real interest in hearing their answers, so overly hasty pacing is most often counter-productive. On the other hand, being too slow can also be extremely frustrating and cause your listener to tune-out. Have you ever waited for what seemed like 10 minutes for someone to ask the next question? You probably wondered if the person had forgotten you completely or was so totally uninterested that coming up with the next question was practically impossible for him. (**Note**: We say "him" here because it's our experience that few women have trouble asking lots of questions! No, we're not chauvinistic, just observant!)

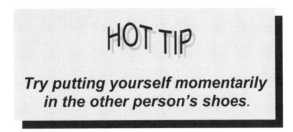

HOT TIP

Try putting yourself momentarily in the other person's shoes.

HOW TO DO IT

▶ Slow down and give the other person time to think! But don't slow down too much or you run the risk of losing attention and creating impatience.

SEQUENCING

In certain situations the answer to one question might influence subsequent questions and answers, making it **SMART** to ask questions in a deliberately specific sequence. Paying attention to sequencing may help you to:

- save time,
- guide the questioning process along certain lines,
- get a specific answer, or
- get a more thoughtful answer.

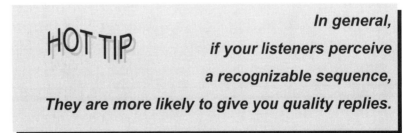

HOT TIP

In general, if your listeners perceive a recognizable sequence, They are more likely to give you quality replies.

Asking Smart Questions

HOW TO DO IT

▶ Consciously use specific types of sequencing.

- Pose questions arranged along a TIME LINE:
    Who was president first Teddy or Franklin Roosevelt?
    What is the final step of the process?

- Ask questions first rooted in the COMFORTABLE or FAMILIAR, then move to the less comfortable/familiar:
    Can you give me some examples of fractions? Then ask,
    What's the difference between proper and improper fractions?

Sequencing is an especially useful technique when you need both general and specific responses. In that kind of situation, you'll find it's often to your advantage to ask general questions first, and then move to more specific, focused questions.

For example, a teenager who can't seem to get her homework turned in on time might be more capable of giving a reasonable answer to a focused (and definitely threatening) question like:

What specific steps do you plan to take to get your assignments turned in? or *How do you plan to clean up your act?*

if she had first worked through some general (lower-threat) questions such as,
Do you understand how to do the assignment?
Would some adjustments in due dates help you meet your deadline?
What might get in the way of the changes you plan to make?
What about trying it the other way around?

Case in Point

Consider the feelings of an injured high school football player. He might be more comfortable talking about the specifics of his options regarding physical therapy or knee surgery than about the threatening general opinion that the injury may ruin his chances of receiving a good scholarship. If you begin with general questions about his doubtful future as a college football star, the answers you receive might not get past vague platitudes. But, if you get him answering questions about the details of his options, other players who faced similar problems in the past, etc., you might succeed in getting candid answers about his feelings when you progress to general questions

Asking Smart Questions

Which process is best? Should you start with general questions and move to specifics, or should you start with specifics and move toward general? You make that decision based on your goal of getting useful, intelligent answers with no teeth pulling involved.

ASSUMPTIONS

Assumptions are a natural part of the communication interaction and they're called into play before a question is even asked. The very fact that you're planning to ask a question indicates you hold at least one 'standard' assumption:

- that what you want to know is knowable.

Without such an assumption as a starting point, the question-asking process couldn't proceed.

And, when you do ask a question, it's easy to assume everyone understand your frame of reference, intent, and meaning. They usually make the same assumption and act on the premise that they are replying within the same context.

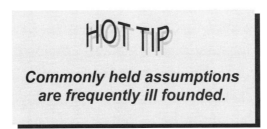

HOT TIP

Commonly held assumptions are frequently ill founded.

Case in Point

Five-year-old Tommy asked his great-grandpa if he could rent a Ninja Turtle video. Tommy just naturally assumed that Gramps knew who the Ninja Turtles were: Everybody knows the Ninja Turtles. He was completely surprised when three minutes into the movie, Gramps accused him of trying to play a trick. Tommy protested; he had not played any tricks. Some further talk and the misunderstanding became clear. How was Tommy to know that old Gramps thought what he was renting was a National Geographic nature film about reptiles in Japan?

Neither Tommy nor Gramps ever thought to check their assumptions. Why should they?

Asking Smart Questions

> **HOT TIP**
>
> *If you don't check the validity of assumptions, (yours and others) you may be in for some interesting surprises!*

⚷ KEY POINT

Assumptions constitute a sort of Chapter Zero.

Case in Point

The US Bureau of Printing and Engraving uses as a slogan *The Buck Starts Here.* If you're a history buff or a US citizen who's old enough to have passed a high school American History class, that's an amusing slogan. But it took one of your authors twenty minutes to clarify it for a couple of ten-year olds visiting Washington, DC! Chapter Zero was missing. The kids 'understood' the slogan as a rather plain sounding statement of the fact that the Bureau prints money. They'd never heard of Truman. Nor did they know what *passing the buck* meant, so *The Buck Stops Here* didn't make much sense, either. At least they realized that in this case a *buck* was a *dollar*. Imagine if we had to go even further back into Chapter Zero!

Chapter Zero is invisible information, usually taken for granted, certainly not needing explanation. Although this all sounds obvious, it unfortunately isn't. Furthermore, because Chapter Zero is invisible information, its non-existence is often never discovered, with baffling mis-communication as a result. Worse yet, it takes a prodigious amount of time to supply Chapter Zero when it *is* discovered to be missing.

Another common type of pre-questioning assumption that can cause major trouble is the presupposition. Questions and their answers are always based on presuppositions, even though we seldom stop to think about them.

For example, if you say that someone speaks English well, your listener will *presuppose* — take it for granted — that the complimented person has a working knowledge of the grammar, vocabulary, and idiomatic usage of the English language. Speaking 'well' could not be accomplished without those elements.

Always check your presuppositions.

HOW TO DO IT

▶ Run a systems analysis check *before* you ask a question.

▶ Ask yourself:

What does the question presuppose?

▶ and second,

Is the presupposition true?

Consider the following famous example:

Is the king of England bald?

The presuppositions here are easy to identify:

1. There is a current king of England.

2. He is either bald or not bald (nothing in between).

If these presuppositions are true, you'll probably get a straightforward yes/no answer. But if there's not a current king of England, or if the king has a seriously receding hairline, but could not really be called either bald or not bald, you will have irremediably confused the issue. If you get any answer at all, it will probably be neither straightforward nor simple.

KEY POINT

For a question to be valid, its presuppositions must be true.

Otherwise, it can't be truly answered. Trying to answer a question with false pre-suppositions forces people into an impossible position. Consider another famous example of this type of problem:

Have you stopped cheating on tests?

Asking Smart Questions

Sometimes indeterminate or false presuppositions serve useful purposes, but only in special circumstances. Think about the questions posed in detective and mystery stories, or by someone trying to get to the root of a problem that's unlikely to yield to normal questioning methods.

> **HOT TIP**
>
> *Unless you are an author of mysteries or an individual responsible for interrogating suspects, beware of questions with false or shaky presuppositions. They will not win you friends or get you unbiased, useful answers.*

Practically speaking, for effective question asking and responding to happen, it is important that everyone concerned understands all the assumptions and presuppositions. If not, you can expect general fogginess.

WORD CHOICE

Selecting appropriate words for the situation and for your listeners is important. For detailed information:

Mental Bungee JUMP
To
Info Site:
Word Choice
page 39

 **INFO SITE**

Word Choice

*. . . you should say what you mean, the March Hare went on.
I do, Alice hastily replied; at least
— at least I mean what I say —
that's the same thing, you know.*

*Not the same thing a bit! said the Hatter.
Why, you might just as well say that
'I see what I eat' is the same thing as 'I eat what I see!'*
— Lewis Carroll

> **HOT TIP**
> Selecting the right words is critical
> to the success of asking good questions.

As Alice found, words can be tricky! One problem is that even basic words often have more than one dictionary meaning. The 500 most commonly used American words have over 14,000 definitions recorded in dictionaries.

*After all, when you come right down to it,
how many people speak the same language
even when they speak the same language?*
— Hoban, Russell

In the face of such multiplicity of meanings, the sad truth is that no matter how many words are available, the ones people use are often inappropriate. Not only that, dictionary meanings change over time. The word "bad" is a good example. Through many centuries of usage, the word was uniformly synonymous with *not good; spoiled, inadequate; disagreeable, ill, distressed* or *unfavorable*:

That is really bad news.
These oranges are bad.
I feel bad.

Asking Smart Questions

But sometime during the last quarter of the Twentieth Century, the word took on a new inflection:

That boy is b-a-a-d.

meaning *the boy is cool; with it; hip* — In other words, *good*! Suppose you, as a parent, were worried about the suitability of a particular child as a playmate. You might ask the teenager next door,

Is that boy as bad as he seems?

If the friendly neighbor defines 'bad' as 'cool', he/she will be answering the wrong question, and you won't find out what you want to know! You would have better luck if you chose more specific words and asked if the boy often misbehaves, or if he gets in trouble in the neighborhood or at school.

> **HOT TIP**
>
> **Make sure your listener understands and answers the question you think you are asking and not some other question altogether!**

Precise Words

Most words carry both denotative (dictionary) and connotative (emotional and value) meanings. In addition, to further complicate matters, words often carry a variety of shades of meaning. So unless you're careful to be precise, your listeners may not grasp the exact meaning you intend. The less precise your word selection is, the greater the opportunity for confusion on the part of your listeners, and the greater the chance you'll not receive an excellent answer.

Words with **double** or **metaphoric** meanings are terrific tools for painting evocative descriptions. But because they conjure up images, they're not quite so useful in asking **SMART** questions.

For example, ***Isn't Jane a pill?*** could mean:

> *Isn't Jane difficult?* or
> *Isn't Jane humorous?* or
> *Isn't Jane delightful?*

Worse yet are button-pushing words — words with strong negative connotations. For example, you may intend merely to suggest that someone has sloppy habits when you ask ***Isn't he a pig?***

Asking Smart Questions

But unfortunately, the word 'pig' pushes buttons. It has too often been used as a pejorative for policemen or to denigrate members of the opposite sex from the speaker. If you're aware that a specific word or phrase carries its own emotional load, you might want to consider choosing another metaphor.

> **HOT TIP**
>
> **By paying attention to the metaphors and/or slang you use, you can help your listeners avoid inferring inaccurate connotations.**

Specific Words

General words refer to an entire category: **cat** Using general words will earn you a vague, general answer. Specific words refer to one representative type within a category: **lion, tiger, tabby,** or **Siamese**. A specific word restricts the meaning, which can be assigned to it — you would never mistake a tiger for a tabby cat! Using specific words will encourage a specific answer.

General: ***Where did you put all that stuff the State Superintendent sent?*** (General Answer: In the teacher workroom.)

Specific: ***Where did you put the sample standardized tests the State Superintendent sent?*** (Specific Answer: In red file folders in a box labeled 'Sample Tests' in the teacher workroom.)

When I use a word, (Humpty Dumpty told Alice) . . .
it means just what I choose it to mean — neither more nor less.
— Lewis Carroll

Asking Smart Questions

Concrete Words

Concrete words refer to objects that are perceived through the senses: *chairs, ice cream, ringing bells.* Abstract words refer to concepts that cannot be perceived through the senses: words such as *freedom, loyalty truth.* Whenever possible, choose *concrete* words in preference to, or at least in conjunction with, abstract words Turn abstract ideas or values into more clearly pictured behavior by using action verbs.

> *Abstract*: *Do you think Blake is careful?*
> *Concrete*: *I see that Blake always proofreads his reports before turning them in — is he that careful about other details?*
> *Concrete*: *Have you noticed that Blake is very careful to support the opinions of some of the less popular people during a group discussion?*

Sexist/Politically Incorrect Words

When you use sexist or other politically incorrect words within a question, you may distort your intended meaning. Worse, you are likely to distract your listeners from your main issue.

In our culture, sexist and other politically incorrect language has been used routinely for so long that it has become not only largely unconscious, but also actually sounds 'better' than newer terms to many people. Becoming sensitive to *your* possible usage is a first step in eliminating such words from your vocabulary and CONSCIOUSLY selecting less inflammatory language.

HOW TO DO IT

▶ If you simply avoid ethnic references, you're unlikely to offend.

▶ If an ethnic reference is necessary, use polite, accepted terminology.

▶ Take care not to trip over sexist language in these two areas:

courtesy and **job titles**, and **personal pronouns**.

Asking Smart Questions

Appropriate Referencing

OK: *Shall I ask my secretary (assistant) to . . . ?*

Not OK: *Shall I ask my girl to . . ?*

OK: *Have you met the author of that book?*

Not OK: *Have you met the Muslim author of that book?*

Similarly, use *lawyer, doctor, poet,* or *actor,* in reference to anyone, regardless of gender or ethnicity, engaged in these occupations.

Courtesy and Job Titles

When in doubt, or as a general rule, use:

Ms. when you don't know a woman's marital status.
Professor when you don't know an individual's highest academic degree
technician or a more *specific title* such as electrician or carpenter, instead of repairman or workman.
specific title instead of businessman.
sales representative instead of 'the woman from Prentice Hall.
chair or **moderator** instead of chairman.

Gender Pronouns

When referring to or writing about specific individuals, use the appropriate gender pronouns:

In <u>his</u> report to the committee, did <u>John</u> mention. . ?
In <u>her</u> report to the committee, did <u>Helen</u> mention . . .?

When not referring to or writing about a specific individual, you have four choices to eliminate sexist generic pronouns — you can use:

Pronoun Pairs: *By what date must <u>each teacher</u> conduct IEP (Individual Education Plan) meetings for <u>his/her</u> special education students?*

Plural form: *By what date must <u>teachers</u> conduct IEP meetings for <u>their</u> special education students?*

Singular form: *By what date must each teacher conduct IEP meetings for special education students?*

'You': *By what date must <u>you</u> conduct IEP meetings for <u>your</u> special education students?*

© 2006 Pieces of Learning

Asking Smart Questions

Jargon

In a professional setting where you are reasonably certain that everyone is using the same jargon, it can be the most efficient method of expressing an idea. Outside of that setting, by its very nature — consisting of words with particular meaning within a specific environment: (professional, religious, recreational) — it's almost certain to create not only confusion, but also extreme irritation for your listener. For example, imagine a conversation in which a psychologist describes to an electrical engineer a lecture she's planning for a group of teenagers:

The whole focus of the talk is to get the kids to give more feedback to their parents, says the psychologist.

Why are you talking about feedback at all? wonders the engineer.

If they're lucky, it won't take too long for them to realize that "feedback" is a jargon word with different meanings in engineering and psychology.

> **HOT TIP**
>
> *Outside of a professional setting, either completely avoid the use of jargon or carefully explain the intended meaning.*

Acronyms

What do you think about SERI's current research?
What can you tell me about NLP?

Could you instantly identify **SERI** as the Solar Energy Research Institute and **NLP** as Neuro Linguistic Programming? The use of *acronyms* — words formed from the initial letters or group of letters in a title or phrase — has become so widespread it's easy to assume that 'everyone' knows what a particular one means. That's usually far from true. If you're trying to ask **SMART** questions, avoid using acronyms without specifying exactly what they mean.

SHORT SENTENCE FORMAT

Regardless of the educational or intelligence level of a listener, long, complex sentences tend to obscure meaning. (That's why Dickens and Thackery are harder to read than the Daily News.)

So, in the interest of clarity, frame questions in a concise and direct fashion. Don't cram everything into one sentence composed of many dependent clauses.

Instead, try using a series of short sentences in constructing your question. That way, your listeners will be more likely to understand what it is you need to know.

And (assuming you've used precise, appropriate, non-sexist, etc., etc. language and followed all the other rules and regulations) they'll be more likely to reward you with useful, intelligent answers the first time around.

Asking Smart Questions

 **INFO SITE**

Question-Asking Alternatives

There are innumerable questions to which the inquisitive mind can . . . receive no answer
—James Boswell

Believe it or not, some people hate asking questions and avoid the entire process whenever possible. And, believe it or not, while there may be no substitute for asking good questions, there *are* other ways to gather information.

HOW TO DO IT

▶ Try some alternative approaches.

COMMENTS and DECLARATIVE STATEMENTS

Straightforward comments and declarative statements may be perceived as less threatening and demanding than direct questioning. This is particularly true in sensitive situations or in conversations among people of diverse cultural backgrounds whose perceptions are not necessarily the same as yours.

Instead of asking a question, you can simply state your opinion, feelings, or knowledge of facts in relation to what has been said. To motivate others to share their opinions and feelings, offer positive, evaluative comments. To elicit explanations or clarifications, express puzzlement.

> **HOT TIP**
> Comments and declarative statements often encourage longer and more complex responses than do questions.

For example, if you were confronted with a stimulus remark like,

> *Well, it's clear that we have no choice but to close an elementary school.*

you might automatically throw a question

> *Why do you say we have no other options? or Based on what hard facts?*

46 © 2006 Pieces of Learning

thereby triggering an equally automatic defensive response. But other options could be more productive:

- **Comment:** *I don't quite understand your reasoning on that point.* (leaves an opening for explanation)

- **Positive Evaluative Comment:** *I agree that Judy Clark has a lot of innovative ideas, but I'm not sure why you intend to vote for her. I thought you disagreed with her position on school closures.* (leaves an opening for sharing opinions and feelings)

- **Declarative Statement**: *I'm not sure that your basic premise is accurate.* (leaves an opening for clarification)

- **Declarative Statement**: *I know, based on the last elections, that the public — and therefore, the school board — is committed to not closing a school.* (leaves an opening for further discussion)

STATEMENTS OF INTEREST

Verbally expressing an interest in what is being said encourages others to continue. It's easy to jump into the conversation with questions such as,

What about . . ? or

Have you considered . . ?

People who like to ask questions may find it difficult to make a simple statement of interest such as:

I'd like to know more about your reasons for thinking that . . .

However, such a statement conveys respect for other people's views, demonstrates your interest, and invites further discussion. Of course, if you aren't interested, silence or a non-committal shrug may be your best options.

HUMOR

Humor is a good tool for lessening emotional stress. When people laugh, the atmosphere is instantly more relaxed and communication flows more freely. For example, after blurting out,

I can't believe you said that — it's so incredibly stupid!

an individual might back off by quipping:

I've been taking Stupid lessons — do you think I'll get an A on the next test?

Asking Smart Questions

> **HOT TIP**
> *Using humor will often cause others to enlarge on ideas and feelings.*

FILLERS

Fillers are minimal verbal or non-verbal responses, such as:

- *mm-humm*
- *yes*
- *I see*
- *OK*
- *good*
- *sure*
- *uh-huh*
- *ahhh*
- nodding your head
- maintaining direct eye contact

Fillers indicate your awareness of what is being said and your willingness to continue listening. They encourage others to continue speaking.

> **HOT TIP**
> *Use fillers when you don't have much to say but want to indicate interest.*

REPETITION

Instead of asking a question such as:

- *What do you mean?* or
- *What are you trying to say?*

use repetition to check your understanding of what has just been said. You can do this in one of two ways:

- **Repeat word for word**

- **Summarize your understanding of the meaning**

The usual response to a repetition or summarization is for the speaker to either agree that you have understood, and then amplify; or, to disagree that you have understood and then clarify.

SILENCES

> *The right word may be effective, but no word was ever as effective as a rightly timed pause.*
> — Mark Twain

> **HOT TIP**
> **Have absolutely nothing to say? Try silence.**

Many people are uncomfortable with any silence in a conversation, discussion, or interview, and feel compelled to say something to 'fill the void'. However, deliberate use of silence can be a very useful tool. Short periods of silence allow others time to think and frame a response. An additional benefit is that others will soon recognize what a good listener you are and may, therefore, be more than willing to talk with you.

> **Note:** If the silence is not of your choosing, and you can't identify any productive outcome as a result, it is a non-deliberate silence. *Non-deliberate* silences are not productive and should, therefore, be avoided. Regain control immediately — by asking questions.

Being able to accept and maintain a comfortable silence is a skill that must be learned and practiced. 'Comfortable' can be defined as a silence lasting about five seconds. How long is five seconds? Find out. Choose a rhyme or lyric you're familiar with and, using a stopwatch, recite or sing it to yourself to see how far you get in five seconds. Practice until you've developed an intuitive feeling for the length of a comfortable silence.

> **HOT TIP**
> **To maintain a 'comfortable' silence, stay actively engaged.**

Asking Smart Questions

HOW TO DO IT

▶ Show you are interested in what has been said and what is to come by maintaining eye contact and using gestures (head nodding, leaning forward, etc.)

Asking Smart Questions

HOME PAGE

Question Types

*A civilized man is one who will give
a serious answer to a serious question.*
— Ezra Pound

A question is a power tool that should be treated as such. Power tools speed and simplify your work. But keep in mind that if you misuse them, they can drill holes in your grandmother's cedar chest or chop off your finger.

Likewise, you may get more (or less) than you bargained for if you use a weed whacker to mow the lawn when an edger is what's needed. Just as there are many types of tools in a workshop — each serving a particular purpose — there are many types of questions. Being a skillful question asker means becoming knowledgeable about the range of possible question types. Then you can efficiently design questions to get the information you want. Failure may not result in misplaced holes or bloody fingers, but it's likely to cause lots of aggravation. For example, it's pointless, time wasting, and frustrating for all concerned if you persist in asking a series of lead-in questions:

Given the evidence, would it be a reasonable guess that the principal might have been kidnapped? If so, aren't we wasting time? Shouldn't we be doing something about it? Isn't there a policy for dealing with this?

when all you really want or need is straight memory-recall of factual information:

What is the procedure for reporting a missing person?

> **HOT TIP**
>
> *The question-asking process is less likely to go awry if it intentionally begins with a choice of question-type.*

© 2006 Pieces of Learning

Asking Smart Questions

CHOOSING USEFUL QUESTIONS

Simply dropping a random question into conversation is wrought with danger! Certainly your goal as a question asker is to choose questions that are useful, so as to receive a sensible, usable answer. Seems pretty obvious — but not all question types are useful and even the ones that are can malfunction if you use them indiscriminately any time, anywhere. And if you don't know which types of questions are generally useful and which are not, you could easily slide into the Non-Productive Question types or even the dreaded X-Rated types — and there go your chances for a worthwhile answer!

So back up and take it one step at a time. The FIRST step in the question-asking process is to determine the *type of question* you want to ask. Choosing a question type is highly dependent on the *INTENT* (or goal) behind the question. For example,

> **What did you mean when you said . . ?**

is a (useful) Clarifying Question if you are asking for a simple explanation. However, said in a different tone of voice, or with other intent, it might really be a Curiosity Question, an Exploration Question, or even a Confronting Question. While these are all useful question types, they will elicit widely different types of answers.

Having a reasonable idea of what kind of response (*factual, emotional, speculative*) and how much of a response you want (*broadly based, narrowly focused, detailed*) will help you ask **SMART** Useful Questions.

Mental Bungee JUMP
To
Home Page:
Useful Questions
Page 59

NON-PRODUCTIVE QUESTIONS

Yes, Non-Productive questions are common! However, they serve no useful purpose as *questions*. There is an entirely different agenda behind asking Non-Productive (pseudo) questions. They are often 'asked' to send a message, to 'sound-off', or to show disagreement. Consider the following:

Asking Smart Questions

> **Case in Point**
>
> Eighteen-year-old Bob came home from a party two hours late and a little the worse for wear. He said he had only had 'a couple of beers,'
>
> His dad exploded — 'How COULD you drink and then drive home? *How many times have we told you: don't drink and drive? What do we have to do to get through your thick skull? You were OK this time but what about the next time? Don't you ever think?*

None of Dad's questions were worthless; they were pertinent, and they sounded as if they were serious questions. But they were Non-Productive Questions because they weren't meant to be answered — at least not during that particular monologue. Can you imagine the result if Bob had tried to answer?

KEY POINT

Questions that are technically 'Non-Productive' often serve a purpose.
Non-Productive doesn't mean the questions shouldn't be used
if circumstances warrant.

➡ **Mental Bungee JUMP**
To
Dictionary:
Non-Productive Questions
Page 114

X-RATED QUESTIONS

X-Rated Questions intentionally sow seeds of discord. They scream hostility and entirely shut down communication. The temptation to use these nasties may, at times seem almost overwhelming — but, as none of them produce useful answers, why bother?

Asking Smart Questions

🗝 KEY POINT

What goes around, comes around . . . The only Results you can expect from X-Rated Questions will be hostile and negative — just like the questions.

There are four main types of X-Rated Questions: While each of the types is different, all types have some characteristics in common.
- None seek an honest answer.
- They're designed to provoke, cause disruption, and embarrass.
- They're often ego enhancement maneuvers motivated by a desire to seek recognition.
- They can be asked to mask ignorance or to cover-up inattention.
- They're sometimes disguised as a 'friendly' comment or 'just a joke'.

HOT TIP

X-Rated Questions cause trouble.
Learn about them. And then avoid them like the plague.

Mental Bungee JUMP
To
Dictionary:
X-Rated Questions
Page 122

 **INFO SITE**

The Basic Six — Plus

I keep six honest serving men
they taught me all I knew:
their names are What and Why
and When and How
and Where and Who
— Rudyard Kipling

When you were in school, you undoubtedly learned about those famous 5W's of question asking: **who, what, when, where**, and **why**. You probably also learned to add some of the basic "H" questions like: **how often, how many, how much, and how to.** You may also have learned to add other refinements like **what if.** All of these are important — they are the building blocks of good questions. Take the time now to do a quick inventory of the basics.

> **HOT TIP**
> 'Quick' really does mean 'Quick' —
> Do this in two minutes, maximum,
> even though the list looks l-o-o-o-ong.

HOW TO DO IT

▶ Use the five W's to run a 'systems analysis' check of your question asking.

- **WHO?** Are you the best person to pose this particular question, or might you get better results if someone else did the asking? There's also the matter of who should *answer*. How many times have you asked a question only to discover you have queried someone who either doesn't know or is unwilling to give an answer? Being an efficient question-asker means judiciously selecting whom you are going to ask.

- **WHAT?** Out of a wide variety of possibilities, you will need to consider what *type* of question will get the most useful response.

Asking Smart Questions

Asking irrelevant, distracting, or not-useful questions is worse than not asking any at all.

Mental Bungee JUMP
To
Home Page:
Question Types
Page 51

- **WHEN?** Timing matters. *Don't be an indiscriminate, question-flinging, conversational boor!* The right time to assess a question's timeliness is before you open your mouth to pose it. Does your need to ask a question warrant an immediate interruption that steps all over a speaker's words? Your question is more likely to be answered appropriately if you first listen to and acknowledge the words of the original speaker.

- **WHERE?** In most cases, the *where* of question asking doesn't mean physical location: it refers to the proper spot in a conversation. (In other words, the *when* and *where* of question asking are usually the same). Occasionally, physical location *does* matter: any parent knows there's both a time and a place for asking a teenager even the simplest of questions!

- **WHY?** Sometimes asking a question might not be the most direct route to finding answers. There are times when asking a question can stop the flow of ideas. For example, in a brainstorming session, question asking definitely gets in the way.

Mental Bungee JUMP
To
Info Site:
Question Asking Alternatives
Page 46

Asking Smart Questions

- **HOW MANY? HOW MUCH? HOW OFTEN?** The most commonly used "how" questions are quantitative. In terms of the question-asking process, *how often* to ask questions is the most important. *How often* to ask questions depends on a lot of things. How curious are you? How great is your need to know? How much do you or don't you understand? Have you asked sixteen questions in the last fifteen minutes? That's probably too many, too often! Five questions in ten minutes? That might still be too many or it might be appropriate to the situation. Just remember that too-frequent questioning can be perceived as threatening or as a substitute for listening.

On the other hand, if you rarely ask questions you can give the impression you are uninterested. So, what to do? What is enough or not enough? That's up to you to figure out. A good way to do it is to pay attention to the nonverbal cues your listeners are giving and adjust accordingly.

NOW FOR THE 'PLUS' PARTS —
Two *Ws* not usually taught in schools — *'Will'* and *'World'*

- **WILL** has to do with intent. It's a refinement of the why question. You must honestly consider it if you want satisfactory results to your question. When your questions aren't aligned with your will, your listeners perceive an underlying dishonesty and communication suffers.

Case in Point	
Parent:	*Why is there a pair of dirty socks on the kitchen table?*
Child:	*I dunno.*
Parent:	*They're obviously your socks, so if you don't know, who does?*
Child:	*I dunno.*

If you're lucky you've never been on either end of an exchange like this, but chances are you may have; it's all too common. Obviously, the parent's primary intent in this conversation was to have the socks removed from the table — the

© 2006 Pieces of Learning

Asking Smart Questions

sooner the better. But the question was not aligned with *"will"*. The child knew the parent had no real interest in hearing about *why* socks were left on the table. So were they promptly removed? NO! Of course not! All that happened was

- a question was asked . . .
- and dutifully "answered" . . .
- and more likely than not, tempers escalated on both sides.

Similar situations occur more frequently than we'd like to think with family, friends and colleagues, so it's important to check your will and consider if it's accurately portrayed in your question.

- **WORLD** It's also important to consider the context (*world*) of your question. A question doesn't exist in a vacuum; it's always part of a communication process. So take a moment to think about how your question fits into the situation. It may make the difference between a timely question and an open-mouth-insert-foot faux pas.

> **HOT TIP**
>
> **Remember Father William's comment in**
> **Alice's Adventures in Wonderland:**
>
> *"I have answered three questions, and that is enough . . .*
> *Do you think I can listen all day to such stuff?"*
> — **Lewis Carroll**

Asking Smart Questions

 **INFO SITE**

Useful Questions

The [useful] questions refuse to be placated . . .
They barge into your life at the times when
it seems most important for them to stay away.

[Useful questions] are the questions
asked most frequently and answered most inadequately
— Ingrid Bengis

A *Useful* question is a question that is honestly seeking an answer — and can, therefore, be answered successfully.

How can you be so stupid? is usually not a useful, answer-seeking question.

What's the homework assignment? usually is.

> **HOT TIP**
>
> *If you don't ask useful questions,*
> *you don't get useful answers.*

Don't worry. There are plenty of useful questions to choose from! Useful questions comprise the largest, most important family of question-types. The family is divided into two main branches: Broad Questions and Specific Questions. The Broad branch has two question-types: Closed and Open-Ended. The Specific Questions branch includes a wide variety of types, any of which could be open questions; many of them could be closed.

Useful questions are versatile and serve multiple purposes. They can:

- **ESTABLISH RAPPORT**

    Would you autograph my copy of last night's newspaper article about the contest winners before I put it up on the bulletin board?

© 2006 Pieces of Learning

Asking Smart Questions

- **STIMULATE INTEREST**

    Did you realize that, according to the 1987 edition of Harper's Index Book, the average American consumes nine pounds of chemical additives per year?

- **SATISFY CURIOSITY**

    How does Chaos Theory help explain the origins of the universe?

- **CLARIFY IDEAS OR ACTIONS**

    Is how to reorganize the flow of traffic in the student parking lot our main problem?

- **UNCOVER OBJECTIONS**

    Would you feel better about it if . . ?

- **PERSUADE**

    Wouldn't the town want to support a state-of-the-art computer lab in the high school?

- **SUMMARIZE IDEAS**

    What have you learned so far about . . ?

Mental Bungee JUMP
To
Dictionary:
Useful Questions
Page 91

 **INFO SITE**

Non-Productive and X-Rated Questions

But oh, beamish nephew, beware of the day,
If your Snark be a Boojum! For then
You will softly and suddenly vanish away,
And never be met with again!
— Lewis Carroll

Non-Productive and X-Rated Questions dwell in the *Seldom-If-Ever* Zone. It's called that for good reason — it's a dark nether-region, full of Boojums. You won't want to visit there. Especially if you have real questions. You won't find any real answers in the *Seldom-If-Ever* Zone.

NON-PRODUCTIVE QUESTIONS

Consider the person in an audience who asks a question by delivering a lecture. The 'question' tacked on to the end of the lecture may seem like a bona-fide question. However, it qualifies as Non-Productive because its purpose most likely had more to do with showing off than getting an answer. Some types of questions (for example, Confirming, Dumb-Smart, and Indirect) are sometimes productive and sometimes not. The difference is the Non-Productive Questions serve no useful *question-asking* purpose even though they may actually be real questions. Question types in the Non-Productive category include:

- ▶ **Confirming:** *I think it's a dumb idea; what do you think?*
- ▶ **Double-Barreled:** *Do you think we should continue the struggle, or should we strike?*
- ▶ **Dumb-Smart:** *This may sound crazy, but couldn't we solve this problem by abolishing the Student Council?*
- ▶ **Implied:** *Phil is sure taking his own time in getting his grade book turned in. (Implied question: When is Phil going to turn in his grade book?)*

Asking Smart Questions

- ▶ **Indirect:** *Everybody complains about having too much homework, so I wonder why you all goof off during study hall.*

- ▶ **Leading:** *You do agree that a small class size is best, don't you?*

- ▶ **Message:** *My research shows that . . . followed by a statement of opinion or fact, and perhaps a brief question.*

- ▶ **Projection:** *Don't you agree that this nonsense about Asking Smart Questions is just that — nonsense?*

Some Non-Productive questions are close kin to X-Rated questions in that they have hidden agendas. Message, Confirming and/or Projection questions are often transparent ploys for group recognition or ego-enhancement. Projection, Dumb-Smart, Double-Barreled, and/or Implied are often attempts at manipulation to gain agreement or to confuse. The motivation behind the Indirect non-productive question seems to be simply avoidance of saying exactly what you mean.

> **HOT TIP**
>
> *Avoid Non-Productive Questions — they're useless.*

X-RATED QUESTIONS

Though sometimes disguised as 'friendly' comments or 'just a joke', X-Rated Questions are hostile. That's all there is to it. They are intentionally designed to provoke, cause disruption, and embarrass. They don't seek honest answers. Sometimes X-Rated Questions are used to mask ignorance or even to cover-up inattention. They never even progress beyond the question mark because they completely, very effectively shut down communication.

There are five main types:

- ▶ **Antagonistic:** *That's nonsense; what on earth do you mean?*

Asking Smart Questions

- ▶ **Black Hole:** *Who do you think you are, smarty-pants — Einstein?*

- ▶ **Gotcha:** *You mean you don't even know . . ?*

- ▶ **Loaded:** *You won't find yourself in this situation again, will you?*

- ▶ **Misleading:** *You're the smartest person I know when it comes to asking questions, not like dumb me. I can't figure it out, but I bet you didn't have any trouble at all with the math homework, did you?*

HOT TIP

What goes around, comes around . . .
The only results you can expect from X-Rated Questions will be hostile and negative — just like the questions.

Mental Bungee JUMP
To
Dictionaries:
Non-Productive – page 114
and
X-Rated
Page 122

Asking Smart Questions

HOME PAGE

Surfing Through the Time Zones

*To everything there is a season,
and a time to every purpose under the heaven . . .*
— Ecclesiastes 3:1–8.

To facilitate the 'how to' part of the question-asking process, we've broken the act of questioning into three basic time zones:

| BEFORE . . . | DURING . . . | AFTER . . . |

a question is asked.

There's also the

| INTERFACE BETWEEN ZONE |

and the not-so-basic

| SELDOM-IF-EVER ZONE |

Becoming aware of the various time zones will help you understand what the question-asking process is all about.

> **HOT TIP**
>
> *Try some Mental Bungee Jumping
> between the various Zones.
> Becoming familiar with the unique aspects of each time zone
> puts you on the road to Asking SMART Questions.*

THE ZONES

Time in the question zones is non-linear — everything sort of happens at once. That's fine when you're used to it. Until then, you'll need to do one thing at a time. Begin at the beginning — enter the Q' Queue (the Question Queue) in the

Before Zone and find out some basic information about question asking. An important element of useful question asking lurks at the Interface between the *Before* Zone and the *During* Zone. Although it's actually the shortest time zone in the question-asking process, the DURING Zone could easily be considered the most important. This is the zone where meaning resides. The *After* Zone is where you find out if you have been successful in asking **SMART** questions. This is where your efforts are either rewarded with answers or ignored.

Mental Bungee JUMP

To

INFO SITES: The *Before* Zone
page 66

INFO SITE: The *Interface* Between The Zones
Page 69

INFO SITE: The *During* Zone
Page 77

INFO SITE: The *After* Zone
Page 82

Note: The *Seldom-If-Ever* Zone isn't a zone you ever *WANT* to be involved with, but you DO need to know about it in order to avoid it.

HOT TIP

Once you've read about all the time zones, you are ready to ask your questions.

Asking Smart Questions

 **INFO SITE**

The *Before* Zone

The time has come, the Walrus said,
To talk of many things:
Of shoes — and ships — and sealing wax —
Of cabbages — and kings —
And why the sea is boiling hot —
And whether pigs have wings.
— **Lewis Carroll**

Step into the Q' Queue and begin your journey into the zones. Proceed with caution: the Q' Queue is no ordinary queue; you can't just stand in it and passively progress to your goal. You have to be active! But it's not a super-highway, either. It's more like a winding road — and it frequently twists back on itself.

> **HOT TIP**
>
> *That's not eerie music you hear —*
> *you're not entering the Twilight Zone.*
> *But to avoid speed traps and potholes,*
> *Learn how to navigate the Q' Queue.*

HOW TO DO IT

▶ Begin in the *Before* Zone. Follow the signs.

The *Before* Zone is where you stop to think about question asking **before** you open your mouth. The actual amount of time spent there, as measured by the clock, isn't much, but it's crucial to **ASKING SMART QUESTIONS**.

What happens, or ought to happen, in the *Before* Zone? Not much, actually. And yet, *lots*. The *Before* Zone is the **Thinking-Zone** of the Q' Queue. It probably seems unnatural to you to do more than voice a question when it pops into your mind. And moving through a Queue of zones probably sounds time-consuming, maybe even more trouble than it could possibly be worth. But wait. Stop for a moment. Consider an example:

Asking Smart Questions

> **Case in Point**
>
> You've probably never thought about the zillions of messages that must pass between your brain and your muscles in the *Before* Zone every time you take a step. But, if for some reason you lost your ability to walk and had to re-learn — ah! Then you'd begin to pay attention to those multiple messages. The task seems nearly impossible. The good news is — it isn't. Many people learn to walk again after an injury. And then — though they gain appreciation for the process, they no longer stop to think how they do it.

It's the same with asking good questions. Right now, you're trying to develop a SKILL, so you need to consciously consider the steps. Once you're aware of all that precedes asking a good question, the process becomes automatic. And then, with new appreciation, you may once again appear to simply voice a question when it pops into your mind.

The first step in the *Before* Zone is determining the type of question you want to ask.

**Mental Bungee JUMP
To
Home Page:
Question Types
Page 51**

When you've pinpointed the type of question you want to ask, you're still not ready to move out of the *Before* Zone. You don't want to just blurt out a question; you want to master the trick of asking a *good* one.

To do that you need to take the second *Before* Zone step: consider (and make appropriate allowances for) the ATTRIBUTES of good questions.

Asking Smart Questions

Mental Bungee JUMP
To
INFO SITE:
Question Attributes
Page 30

The Good News

You've come to the end of the *Before Zone*.

The Interesting News

There are three more zones you need to visit before you become a Master Question Asker.

> **HOT TIP**
>
> Skip the *Before Zone* Info Sites
> AT YOUR PERIL.
> *You may find yourself
> "madly (trying to) squeeze
> a right-hand foot into a left-hand shoe."*
> — Lewis Carroll

 **INFO SITE**

The *Interface* Between the *Before* and *During* Zones

Time is everything: Five minutes makes the difference between victory and defeat.
— Horatio Nelson

Once you understand the *Before* Zone, it's time to move on. But you can't move directly into the *During* Zone. Remember, the Q' Queue twists and turns, and time in the question zones is non-linear.

An important element of useful question asking lurks at the **between** the *Before* and the *During* Zones of question asking. Unfortunately, there's no yellow, diamond-shaped DANGER sign at the Interface. There ought to be. Or at the very least, a warning: **SLIPPERY WHEN WET** to put you on notice that this is a tricky interchange.

What makes it tricky? The *Interface* between the *Before* and the *During* Zones has to do with the difference between messages and meta-messages.

MESSAGES AND META-MESSAGES

*You see, it's like a portmanteau —
there are two meanings packed up into one word.*
— Lewis Carroll

Questions, like most of what we say, operate on at least two content levels at once. They simultaneously deliver a **message** and a **meta-message.**

The **message** is the easy part to understand. It's the straightforward content, usually a request for some kind of information, just what you would expect a question-message to be. However, many questions are more complex, containing a **meta-message**, or secondary level of meaning. The meta-message conveys equally important information, but because it's subtle, it's sometimes ignored or misinterpreted.

There are several different types of meta-messages that might be embedded within a question. We use them all of the time, mostly unconsciously. They are a combination of *Before* Zone elements and some nonverbal *During* Zone elements, projecting information about relationships, values, and attitudes (toward others and the situation). In addition, they frequently establish both the climate

Asking Smart Questions

and the basis of the communication interaction. You might be wondering how so many meta-messages could be slipped into one, innocent-sounding question. It's not at all difficult. Has anyone ever told you your **Attitude** was showing?

- Do you know people who always sound as though they're *complaining* even if that's not their intention?

- Do you sometimes respond negatively to even well intentioned *criticism*? Is it the words that tend to upset you or the nonverbal behaviors that accompany the words?

- Do you ever put an *emotional load* on a question you're asking?

- Do you feel annoyed when people in positions of authority slide *indirect orders* into a conversation?

- Do you ever deliberately *emphasize* certain **words** to make a point or to convey meaning?

> **HOT TIP**
> Since meta-messages frequently establish both the climate and the foundation of communication, find out how they influence question asking —
> Then learn to make them work FOR you instead of against you.

ATTITUDE

Questioners show their attitudes through non-verbal behaviors such as voice-tone, gestures, and facial expressions. Regardless of what the words *seem* to mean, the *attitude* behind the words will color the perceived meaning. For example, suppose you ask,

> ***How did you arrive at such an interesting conclusion?***

Depending on your attitude, your listener could interpret your meaning in several different ways: you meant that the conclusion

- **is really interesting.**
- **is really stupid.**

- **is very strange.**
- **will never be accepted.**

> **HOT TIP**
> *To be certain your WORDS are received as you intend, make sure your ATTITUDE reflects your intention.*

COMPLAINING

Some chronic complainers don't seem to know how to defend or explain themselves without making complaints an integral part of the process. But even non-complainers may fall prey to the temptation to complain if they feel themselves under personal attack.

What's wrong with the way I handled the meeting?

may be an honest request for information, but it's only a small whine away from being a complaint. And complaints can completely distort your intended meaning. Extreme caution is needed to keep the meta-message from taking over in a situation where a complaint might lurk so close to the surface.

> **HOT TIP**
> *Questions asked in a non-judgmental manner sound more like questions and less like complaints — and are more likely to get useful answers.*

CRITICISM

Classically, 'criticism' means analyzing and making judgments, both positive and negative. But in our everyday language usage, criticism has largely lost its positive connotations. Knowing that *negative* criticism makes others uncomfortable, people are often tempted to hide it by embedding it in an otherwise innocuous question. Unfortunately, this tactic is usually recognized for what it is and is likely to cause more anger than a straightforward negative comment.

Asking Smart Questions

> **Case in Point**
>
> Before her husband and son headed out for a baseball game, Jane asked them to pick up some milk on the way home. They came back late in the afternoon, excited about the game, talking a mile a minute, and conspicuously empty-handed.
>
> ***Did you remember to pick up the milk?*** was Jane's greeting.

As the answer was patently obvious, that was no innocent question — it was classic covert criticism. We suspect that the 'climate' of the next few minutes would probably keep the non-existent milk well refrigerated. What do you think?

Note: People are often sensitive to criticism of *any* kind — both negative and positive.

EMOTIONAL LOAD

A question's emotional load can dramatically — and dangerously — complicate its apparent surface meaning. It happens between parents and teenagers on a regular basis.

> **Case in Point**
>
> Susan and her teenage daughter, Beth, had an all too typical conversation: When Susan reminded Beth that her presence was expected, Beth asked an apparently straightforward, information-seeking question: ***Why do I have to go?***
>
> Susan's knee-jerk response to her daughter was: ***Because you're part of this family and this is a family event and that's all there is to it!***
>
> Beth was equally quick: ***I'm sick of family events!***

Sound at all familiar? The problem arises because of the emotional load Beth's 'question' carries. It was asked in such a way as to convey, in no uncertain terms, not a request for information, but rather that she wanted no part of either 'old folks' or extended-family gatherings. Beth set her mother up for a fast, emotion-laden exchange — which is exactly what she got. But if, rather than couching her objections in a pseudo-question, she had stated her preferences in a straightforward manner, she likely would have received a gentler response:

But Uncle Elliot would be disappointed if you weren't there.

> **HOT TIP**
>
> *Defuse the emotionally loaded time bomb; avoid pseudo-questions.*

INDIRECT ORDERS

What child hasn't learned an unpleasant lesson by answering,

"No, not right now, I'm busy."

when a parent 'asks'

Could you take out the trash?

Orders, especially indirect ones, abound in our relationships with others. Think of any hierarchical relationship — employer/employee, teacher/student, parent/child — and sooner or later an indirect order will be issued, most often in the guise of a question.

> **HOT TIP**
>
> *Avoid asking indirect questions — they can pull you into a whirlpool of misunderstanding and argument.*

Asking Smart Questions

WORD EMPHASIS

Whether consciously or unconsciously, word emphasis is voiced in all messages. The emphasis you give to particular words within a message can either enhance or cloud the meaning of the message you want to send. It WILL (perhaps unintentionally on your part) influence the response you get.

> **HOT TIP**
>
> The answer to the question,
> "Does it matter HOW questions are asked"? is
> Without question!

HOW TO DO IT

▶ Be aware of the emphasis you place on your words so you send the message you intend.

▶ Try these quick exercises and you'll see the point:
Read the following questions *ALOUD*. Emphasize only the word indicated by bold type and caps, and see what a difference it makes. Notice how word emphasis changes the meaning of the question.

WELL, what do you make of that?

Well, WHAT do you make of that?

Well, what DO you make of that?

Well, what do YOU make of that?

Well, what do you make of THAT?

Now read the next set of questions aloud. Stress EITHER the words **should** and **will** or **not**. You'll find you can subtly control the response.

Do you think our school district SHOULD or SHOULD NOT have a special program for the gifted and talented?

Do you think the weak dollar and slowing economy WILL or WILL NOT have a serious long-term effect on blue chip stocks?

Clearly, there are many different levels of communication that can be layered into a question. Here's a chart that illustrates how different types of meta-messages might be embedded within an apparently straightforward question.

A COMPARISON

STRAIGHT FORWARD MESSAGE	POSSIBLE META-MESSAGE	TYPE
What seems to be the problem?	Could be a show of concern or annoyance, depending on attitude.	Attitude
Why do you say/feel/think?	You always make a big deal out of nothing.	Complaint
Why are you doing that?	That is really a dumb thing to do.	Criticism
Why do you want to watch those reruns?	I don't want to watch this program; I'm bored.	Emotional Load
What are you doing?	Don't do that!	Indirect Order
How do you feel about the way Jim handled that problem?	Could be an entirely different question depending on whether "do," "you," "way," or "Jim" was emphasized.	Word Emphasis

That's nothing to what I could say if I chose, the Duchess replied.
— Lewis Carroll

Asking Smart Questions

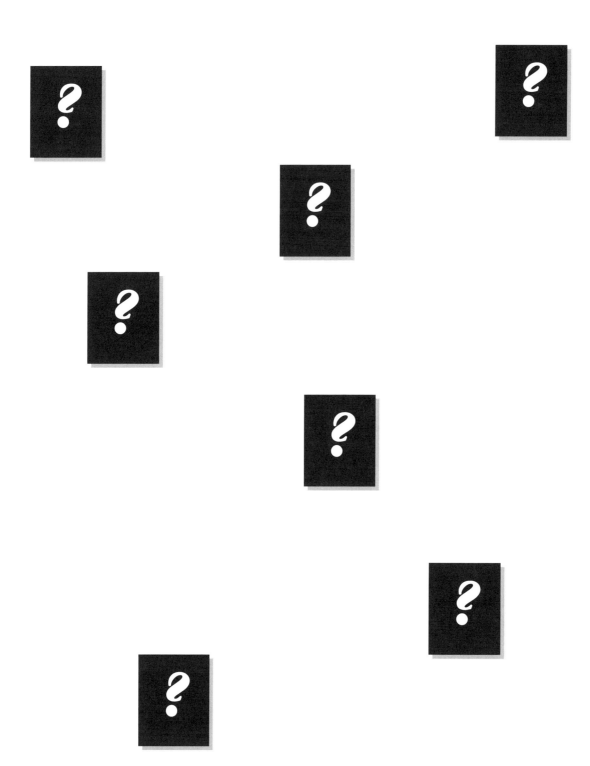

 **INFO SITE**

The *During* Zone

*Every question we answer leads on to another question.
This has become the greatest survival trick of our species.*
— Desmond Morris

Although it's actually the shortest time zone in the question asking process, the *During* Zone could easily be considered the most important. After all, the point of the entire question-asking process happens here! This is the zone where meaning resides — where **HOW** you ask your question is vitally important.

CREATING THE CLIMATE

Is there in the world a climate more uncertain than our own?
— William Congreve

It's often said of Colorado (and, undoubtedly of many more locales) that 'if you don't like the weather, wait a few minutes!' In question asking, you can go one better: if you don't like the climate, change it. Your overall attitude as a questioner sets the communication climate. It determines the type of question you ask, the actual words you choose, and the nonverbal messages you send.

It pays to spend some time establishing an appropriate question-asking climate. In most situations, you'll want to build rapport and create a friendly atmosphere as soon as possible. If your questions come across as an attack (actual or veiled), or, if you appear uninterested, the 'climate' will be cold. In either case, the responses you receive may be of very little use. If, on the other hand, you create a climate of courtesy, understanding, and respect, you'll encourage non-defensive, open responses.

> **Research Report**
> Surprisingly, even interrogators investigating a crime find that a non-judgmental climate of courtesy, understanding, and respect earns them more complete and honest answers than they get with hostility and intimidation. Relaxed, non-defensive people are able to participate more fully than those who, for whatever reason, are afraid to reply.
>
> **Dillon, 1990**

Asking Smart Questions

Climate plays a major role in how people feel. But we aren't completely at the mercy of Mother Nature. We can and do create our own emotional climates. Knowing that, take care.

HOW TO DO IT

▶ Run a 'systems analysis' check. Ask yourself the following questions:

- **Why am I asking this particular question?**

If your reply is that you need an answer, then the question is likely appropriate. If not, perhaps a paraphrase or a statement would be better than a question. An inappropriate question used, for example, merely to prolong a discussion, or worse, to discredit someone, is an instant climate destroyer.

- **If I were on the other end of this question, would I feel the questioner could be trusted?**
- **Am I capable of explaining myself in this situation?**
- **Would I be reasonably comfortable answering the question?**

If you answer an unqualified YES to all three questions, you have probably created a healthy climate.

- **Is my questioning attitude *congruent* with the type of questions I'm asking and *consistent* with my purpose?**

You wouldn't giggle and poke a recent college graduate in the ribs while asking, *'What do you think of your chances of finding a job in your field when companies all over the country are determinedly down-sizing?'* Not if you wanted a real answer!

NON-VERBAL MESSAGES

A wise old owl sat on an oak,
The more he saw the less he spoke;
The less he spoke the more he heard;
Why aren't we like that wise old bird?
— Edward H. Richards

You wouldn't think that things you DON'T say could influence the climate, and therefore, the response you'll get to your question, would you? It's true, though: the nonverbal cues you send significantly influence what happens next. Would you give a detailed answer to someone who didn't even look up from the newspaper when asking, *'How was your meeting'*? Would you feel comfortable if your bridge partner violently threw his cards on the table while quietly saying, *'No, I'm NOT upset'*?

Research Report

Some researchers assert that a listener receives 65 percent of the meaning of any message non-verbally. Others claim as much as *98 percent* of messages are perceived non-verbally.

So somewhere between 2 and 35 percent of the *received* meaning is derived from the actual, spoken words.

HOW you ask a question or give an answer is all-important because your nonverbal behaviors will reveal your REAL intended meaning (even if you're not fully aware of it yourself).

The Interesting News

If there's a contradiction between the verbal and nonverbal parts of a message, people will most often believe the nonverbal.

Understanding the content of messages is usually dependent on nonverbal aspects — a facial expression, a shrug of a shoulder, or a gesture can change the meaning of your message. However, there are no guarantees that listeners will interpret nonverbal cues the way the sender intended.

Asking Smart Questions

Of course, no one way of expressing a question will be appropriate for all types of questions in all types of situations. But your progress along the Q' Queue toward results will be less frustrating if you learn more about how nonverbal behavior influences listeners' perceptions.

> **HOT TIP**
> *Nonverbal/Verbal alignment enhances meaning and intent.*

This may sound complicated, but it all boils down to —

To increase the probability of receiving a quality answer, carefully match your words and your non-verbal behavior, so that your interest in the response is as obvious as possible.

HOW TO DO IT

▶ Use natural gestures.

▶ Develop your ability to easily establish and maintain eye contact.

▶ AVOID a reporter's tone of 'Just give me the facts, right now.'

Asking Smart Questions

> **Warning Label**
>
> BEFORE you invest time and energy studying nonverbal behavior (your own and/or that of others) . . . Read the fine print (specially magnified here for your benefit):
>
> *. . . no two people see the external world*
> *in exactly the same way.*
> *To every separate person*
> *a thing is what he thinks it is — in other words,*
> *not a thing, but a think.*
> — Penelope Fitzgerald
>
> Nonverbal communication is, by nature, ambiguous. Interpretation of nonverbal messages is an art, not a science. It's inaccurate to assign 'truth' to any particular nonverbal behavior. Even though nonverbal behaviors can be revealing, many possible interpretations exist for any given behavior. For example, arms crossed over the chest don't necessarily signal rejection; they could simply mean the person is feeling physically cold.

This time it (the Cheshire Cat) vanished quite slowly,
beginning with the end of the tail,
and ending with the grin,
which remained some time after the rest of it had gone.
— Lewis Carroll

Asking Smart Questions

 **INFO SITE**

The *After* Zone

Is there any thing beyond? — who knows?
— Witter Bynner

Getting answers is the purpose for which questions are asked, but too often questioners assume that all they have to do is ask, and they'll automatically get good answers. If that were the case, you wouldn't need to put so much energy into framing good questions! What's more, even after you frame a good question, there's one last question-asking time zone to think about.

The *After* Zone is the final time zone of the question-asking process, where your efforts are either rewarded with answers or spurned.

Hold it! How can the *After* Zone be PART of the process?
Doesn't it come AFTER question asking?

Usually that's the case. But, the wrap-up *is* part of the process. This is where everything comes together. This is where you find out if you've really been ASKING *SMART QUESTIONS*. If you haven't, you'll know — you'll feel as though you'd passed *Through the Looking Glass* instead!

Note: Sometimes, no matter how carefully you frame a question, you don't get the kind of answer you need. If that happens, DON'T give up. Even Alice had to try more than one technique!

HOT TIP

*All answers are not equal.
Learn some Poor Answer Prevention
and Coping Techniques.*

Mental Bungee JUMP
To
INFO SITE:
Re-Phrasing Poor Questions
Page 133

The final step is so simple it hardly bears mentioning — LISTEN to the answer when you get it. Surprisingly, this is an often neglected step!

It's the oldest rule in the book, said the King.
Then it ought to be Number One, said Alice.
— Lewis Carroll

Mental Bungee JUMP
To
INFO SITE:
Listening In The Time Zones
Page 128

Asking Smart Questions

 **INFO SITE**

The *Seldom-If-Ever* Zone

"Beware the Jabberwock, my son!
The jaws that bite, the claws that catch!
Beware the Jubjub bird, and shun
The frumious Bandersnatch!"
— Lewis Carroll

You'll need the *'vorpal sword'* Carroll recommends for slaying Jabberwocks if you venture into the *Seldom-If Ever*-Zone. It's populated with the nasty cousins of **SMART** questions — the X-Rated Questions. And they bite.

> **HOT TIP**
> *Protect yourself against stumbling unaware into one of the unsociable inhabitants of the Seldom-If-Ever Zone types.*

Have you ever played the silly game in which, whatever you do, you must not think of a white elephant? Of course, once the suggestion is made, it's impossible to avoid — especially when you see an entire Dictionary devoted to them (and labeled X-Rated in the bargain!). Unfortunately, the *Seldom-If-Ever* Zone is well populated with the nasty cousins of SMART questions.

> **HOT TIP**
> You should
> NEVER, EVER, enter this zone.

Hearing that, something approaching 110% of readers will proceed immediately to the X-Rated Dictionary! (It's very difficult to avoid this often unrecognized and possibly misunderstood category of questions.) So, at the least, protect yourself against stumbling into one of the unsociable inhabitants of the *Seldom-If-Ever* Zone types unaware.

Asking Smart Questions

HOW TO DO IT

▶ Go ahead: the last step in fully understanding and appropriately using the family of Useful Questions is to examine their opposites.

**Mental Bungee JUMP
To
Dictionary:
X-Rated Questions
Page 122**

Asking Smart Questions

HOME PAGE

 # The Dictionaries

The Only Dumb Question is the Question You Don't Ask.
— **Roadside Billboard**

Some people, like Henry Higgins in *My Fair Lady,* are content to mutter and wail, *'Why can't a woman be more like a man?'* or some other variation on the general theme that people are different. Others intuitively try to vary their question-asking style to match the needs and/or thinking styles of their listeners.

Professor Higgins never quite got it; he could only operate in a single mode. Eliza had more than one way to think about a subject, and was, therefore, able to engineer a happy ending to their story.

HOT TIP — *Be an Eliza.*

HOW TO DO IT

▶ Put on a proverbial 'thinking cap' and learn how to consciously adjust your thinking and questioning styles to specific people or situations.

But be careful — you wouldn't normally wear a fishing hat to church. Just as you could choose to wear a cowboy hat, a baseball cap, or a straw boater depending on your mood or need, you can figuratively choose to wear a specific Thinking Cap depending on the kind of thinking you want to do, the type of question you want to ask, and the type of person you're questioning.

Still, a Thinking Cap is merely a prop — what really matters is what's going

Asking Smart Questions

on underneath. If your thinking is fuzzy or in a rut, your questions will be, too. And, fuzzy, rut-bound questions beget fuzzy, rut-bound answers. What to do?

To ask **SMART** questions, you have to engage your **SMARTS**. (And yes, **SMARTS** are plural!) Glenn Capelli of the True Learning Centre in Perth, Australia, describes four Key Smarts for **SMART** question asking:

- Analytical **SMARTS** — used when you want to approach question asking from an *Investigator* and/or a *Judge* stance. *(A Sherlock Holmes-style tweed Thinking cap would be appropriate.)*

- Relationship **SMARTS** — used when a *Teacher* and/or a *Partner* attitude would best serve. *(A snap-brim hat adjusts to different angles — perfect for a Relationship Thinking cap.)*

- Creative **SMARTS** — used when you want to approach question asking with an *Explorer* and/or *Mystic* style. *(A beret-style Thinking cap might aid creativity.)*

- Practical **SMARTS** — used when a *Manager* and/or *User* perspective is appropriate. *(A southwester might be a practical Thinking cap.)*

Useful question types in each of the four Key **SMARTS** are:

Analytical	Relationship	Creative	Practical
Analysis	Clarifying	Conjecture	Action
Evaluative	Confronting	Curiosity	Application
Probing	Connection	Exploration	Policy
Synthesis	Value	Hypothetical	Translation
Verification			

To find these and more —

Mental Bungee JUMP
To
The Dictionaries
Page 86

© 2006 Pieces of Learning

Asking Smart Questions

Questionnaire: What Type of Question Asker Am I?

The easiest person to deceive is one's self.
— Edward Bulwer-Lytton

DIRECTIONS: Answer the following questions, remembering there are no right or wrong answers. Check no more than two statements in each set. For best results, cover the question type (Analytical, Coach, Practical, etc.) while you are selecting your answers.

1. In general, when I ask a question, I am most interested in
    - ___ a. identifying and challenging assumptions underlying thoughts and actions. (Analytical)
    - ___ b. exploring a topic in depth. (Analytical)
    - ___ c. knowing how I can use the answer. (Practical)
    - ___ d. encouraging expansion of ideas and feelings. (Relationship)
    - ___ e. stimulating thought about a question. (Coach)
    - ___ f. exploring new ways to think about the subject. (Creative)

2. In general, when I ask a question, I'm looking for an answer that gives me
    - ___ a. the facts, just the facts. (Practical)
    - ___ b. exciting possibilities to consider. (Creative)
    - ___ c. clarification of points made earlier. (Coach)
    - ___ d. an understanding of my position in relation to others. (Relationship)
    - ___ e. an interpretation of the situation. (Analytical)
    - ___ f. immediate, useful feedback. (Practical)

3. In general, when I ask a question, I want
    - ___ a. to get the facts straight. (Practical)
    - ___ b. to get others to accept my values and beliefs. (Relationship)
    - ___ c. to analyze the situation. (Analytical)
    - ___ d. to 'stir the pot', get others excited and curious. (Relationship)
    - ___ e. to stimulate a brainstorming approach. (Creative)
    - ___ f. to facilitate discussion. (Coach)

Asking Smart Questions

Questionnaire: What Type of Question Asker Am I?

4. Faced with an urgent problem to solve, I tend to ask questions that will help me

    ___a. get quickly to 'the bottom' of the situation. (Practical)
    ___b. initiate a discussion on the topic. (Coach)
    ___c. bring difficult subjects into open discussion. (Relationship)
    ___d. focus on the consequences of a proposed solution. (Practical)
    ___e. facilitate brainstorming. (Creative)
    ___f. judge whether a proposed action should be taken. (Analytical)

5. In almost any situation. I tend to select questions that will be most likely to help me

    ___a. approach the topic in a round-about manner in order to lessen any sense of threat. (Relationship)
    ___b. identify the strengths and weaknesses of a proposed course of action. (Practical)
    ___c. stimulate creative thinking. (Creative)
    ___d. determine the relative worth of a proposed solution. (Analytical)
    ___e. guide others toward a fruitful discussion. (Coach)
    ___f. establish the parameters of the situation. (Analytical)

6. Working with others to solve a problem, I tend to select questions that will be most likely to help me

    ___a. define terms in order to ensure that the meanings are understood in the same way by everyone. (Analytical)
    ___b. encourage others to explain their ideas. (Coach)
    ___c. apply what I know about a similar situation. (Practical)
    ___d. reach consensus. (Relationship)
    ___e. explore alternative solutions. (Creative)
    ___f. analyze elements that led to or created the problem. (Analytical)

7. When I want to develop a personal relationship, I tend to select questions most likely to help me

    ___a. encourage expansion of ideas and feelings by others. (Coach)
    ___b. clarify a concept or a previous answer. (Analytical)
    ___c. expand on questions that ask: *what if*. (Creative)
    ___d. create a positive climate. (Relationship)
    ___e. focus on the 'here and now' of building the relationship. (Practical)
    ___f. put the other person at ease. (Relationship)

© 2006 Pieces of Learning

Asking Smart Questions

Questionnaire: What Type of Question Asker Am I?

8. Studying a new subject in a group situation, I tend to ask questions, which will be most likely to help me

   a. take an idea, process, or situation apart so that the component parts can be separately examined. (Analytical)
   b. build connections between ideas. (Creative)
   c. translate a detailed report into a brief summary or outline. (Coach)
   d. reveal personal biases based on individual values. (Relationship)
   e. initiate a plan of how to learn the subject (Practical)
   f. create a positive climate for learning. (Relationship)

9. Studying a new subject by myself, I tend to ask myself questions, which will be most likely to help me

   a. address such issues as the value or importance of the subject. (Creative)
   b. stimulate my interest. (Coach)
   c. transfer abstract theory into practical application. (Analytical)
   d. apply the new information to what I already know. (Practical)
   e. identify how I feel about the subject. (Relationship)
   f. motivate, initiate, or modify my behavior. (Coach)

10. If I find myself in the middle of an uncomfortable, stalled conversation and wish to resolve the situation, I tend to ask questions, which help me

    a. think aloud — not necessarily seeking an answer — but rather to get others to think about the situation. (Coach)
    b. move someone out of what seems like an untenable position. (Relationship)
    c. decipher a previous unclear response. (Analytical)
    d. focus on differences in opinions, beliefs, attitudes. (Relationship)
    e. get the conversation back 'on track'. (Practical)
    f. envision a new or unique direction. (Creative)

Interpretation: List how many of each type of question you marked:

_____ Analytical

_____ Coach

_____ Creative

_____ Practical

_____ Relationship

What is your primary questioning style? How can you develop additional styles?

INFO SITE

Dictionary of Useful Questions

> **HOT TIP**
> *Useful questions are those that must be honestly answer seeking. They can, therefore, be answered successfully.*

ACTION QUESTIONS

DESCRIPTION Action questions focus on *doing*. They are process-oriented.

WORDING EXAMPLES

What might be the first step toward solving the problem?

Specifically, how can you organize your ideas into a well-written essay?

PURPOSES

- ▶ to motivate, initiate, or modify behavior.
- ▶ to focus attention on actions.
- ▶ to initiate a plan of action.

ACTION QUESTIONS

- ▶ can be used to get a discussion moving again after it has stalled.
- ▶ facilitate development of a step-by-step solution.

🕷 BUGS and ↳ TROUBLE SHOOTING

- 🕷 Pushing *too hard* for a solution.
- 🕷 Pushing *too soon* for a solution.
    - ↳ In each case wait for the appropriate moment.

Asking Smart Questions

ANALYSIS QUESTIONS

DESCRIPTION Analysis questions are used to take an idea, process, or situation apart so that the component parts can be separately examined. They are the opposite of synthesis questions.

WORDING EXAMPLES

What were the main contributing factors that led to the Civil War?

Do you understand the relationship between your problems with the substitute and the need for you to make a written list of the dos and don'ts of classroom behavior?

PURPOSES

- **to discover the nature or function of, or the relationships between, various parts of a whole.**
- **to assess the value or usefulness of solving a problem.**

ANALYSIS QUESTIONS

- tend to be penetrating questions.
- require specifics in the answer.
- often contain words such as *component parts, contributing factors, impact on*, and *relationship between*.

🕷 BUGS and ↳ TROUBLE SHOOTING

- 🕷 Over-generalizing.
    - ↳ Don't neglect to analyze the current situation simply because a given solution has worked in the past.
- 🕷 Not considering all factors.
    - ↳ Slow down and look at the situation from as many angles as possible.
- 🕷 Misunderstanding or misusing the reasoning process.
    - ↳ Focus on one aspect of the situation at a time.

APPLICATION QUESTIONS

DESCRIPTION Application questions are designed to facilitate transferring skills or knowledge from one situation to another.

WORDING EXAMPLES

How can you use what you've learned about geometry to make a simple fractal using triangles?

How can we use the questioning techniques we have learned to solve this mystery?

PURPOSES

- ▶ to take knowledge of principles or generalizations pertinent to a familiar situation and apply them to a similar, but unfamiliar situation.
- ▶ to transfer abstract theory into practical application.
- ▶ to solve problems by using appropriate generalizations and skills.

APPLICATION QUESTIONS

- ▶ often begin with *how* or *in what way*.
- ▶ may deal with the application of very specific details, or
- ▶ may deal with the application of an entire process or idea without worrying about the nitty-gritty specifics.

🕷 BUG and ↳ TROUBLE SHOOTING

🕷 Not making the connections between familiar and new contexts clear.

↳ Use words related to both halves of the connection you want to make.

Asking Smart Questions

CLARIFYING QUESTIONS

DESCRIPTION Clarifying questions are most often follow-up questions used to simplify complex issues or to decipher an unclear response.

WORDING EXAMPLES

What did you mean when you said . . ?

Is it correct that your group is working together to gather information, but you each have specific responsibilities for the final presentation?

PURPOSES
- ▶ **to facilitate examination of objectives.**
- ▶ **to seek detailed explanations.**
- ▶ **to help prevent misunderstanding.**
- ▶ **to seek a definition of terms or phrases and to ensure that the meanings are understood in the same way by everyone.**
- ▶ **to slow down and re-examine an issue.**

CLARIFICATION QUESTIONS
- ▶ may require paraphrasing of earlier questions or answers so that your intended meaning is clearly understood.
- ▶ should be stated in specific terms.
- ▶ may, if overused, make you appear manipulative or bossy.

🕷 BUGS and ↪ TROUBLE SHOOTING

🕷 Sounding like you're challenging rather than questioning.
  ↪ Choose neutral words and be careful of your tone of voice.

🕷 Straying from the main topic; leading into side issues.
  ↪ Stick to one topic at a time.

🕷 Making a nuisance of yourself by asking a series of ever-narrower Clarifying Questions due to impatience.
  ↪ Listen to the entire answer before you ask another question.

Asking Smart Questions

CLOSED QUESTIONS

DESCRIPTION Closed questions require specific information. Frequently they use a yes/no, true/false or multiple-choice format.

WORDING EXAMPLES

Do you know where the band room is?

When is make-up work due?

PURPOSES

- ▶ to elicit a specific response.
- ▶ to restrict the topic and narrow the choice of answers.
- ▶ to discourage further amplification.

CLOSED QUESTIONS

- ▶ are characterized by several introductory words or phrases: the standard *who, what, when,* and *where,* as well as *do,* and *are you* (or *were you, have you, will you,* or *can you*).
- ▶ should be used sparingly. Asking several closed questions in a row makes you sound like the Grand Inquisitor, and thereby inhibits the type and amount of information you will receive.
- ▶ are most efficient when you make the possible alternative replies clear.
- ▶ have the advantage of focusing attention on the most relevant aspects.
- ▶ have the disadvantage of possibly unnecessarily limiting the response.
- ▶ are sometimes characterized as "dead-end" questions.

🕷 BUGS and ↳TROUBLE SHOOTING

🕷 Phrasing the question so that it could have more than one answer.

  ↳ Make the range of acceptable answers clear.

🕷 Asking a closed question (thereby limiting the information you get) when that is not your real intent.

  ↳ Ask follow-up question that focus on relevant details.

© 2006 Pieces of Learning

Asking Smart Questions

CONFRONTING QUESTIONS

DESCRIPTION Confronting questions are used in situations where gentler methods might be ineffective.

WORDING EXAMPLES

How do you explain the fact that the two of you worked this problem in exactly the same wrong way?

Do you understand the penalties for plagiarism?

PURPOSES

- ▶ to bring difficult subjects into open discussion.
- ▶ to focus on differences in opinions, beliefs, attitudes.
- ▶ to precipitate action.

CONFRONTING QUESTIONS are most helpful when

- ▶ the accompanying nonverbal cues are non-aggressive and low key.
- ▶ they are preceded by an *'I'* statement rather than a *'You'* statement.
- ▶ your determination to seek a solution is made plain with an *'I want to reach a solution, but I won't be pushed around'* stance.

Note: People are often unwilling to use confronting questions for fear of inciting conflict. However, using them carefully in a positive and constructive manner can actually reduce conflict.

🕷 BUGS and ↳ TROUBLE SHOOTING

🕷 Projecting aggression so that only defensive responses are offered.
   ↳ Confront the issue, not the person.

🕷 Creating so much dissension that all discussion is stopped.
   ↳ Avoid name-calling and finger pointing. Confronting questions don't necessarily need to be negative.

Asking Smart Questions

CONJECTURE QUESTIONS

DESCRIPTION Conjecture questions ask for an educated guess or opinion about future possibilities.

WORDING EXAMPLES

What's the probability of Maude becoming our principal?

Do you think Main Street Computers would donate some K-3 software for the new computer lab?

PURPOSES

- ▶ **to anticipate problems, trends, needs, or demands.**
- ▶ **to focus on probabilities.**
- ▶ **to focus on consequences or long term effects.**
- ▶ **to bring others into agreement with your position.**

CONJECTURE QUESTIONS

- ▶ often begin with words like 'what if, will, should, could and suppose'.
- ▶ often lead to a follow-up question.
- ▶ can be used to initiate problem solving.
- ▶ are good for stimulating creative thinking.
- ▶ are often solidly based in current reality.
- ▶ are useful persuasion tools; help point out strengths/weaknesses in positions.
- ▶ can facilitate the opening up of a discussion for a compromise.

🕷 BUGS and ↳ TROUBLE SHOOTING

- 🕷 Basing the question on wishful thinking.
- 🕷 Ignoring past experience.
    - ↳ Do reality checks with your data.
- 🕷 Basing the question on an insufficient database.
    - ↳ Remember that 'conjecture' doesn't necessarily mean going off into the 'wild blue yonder'.

© 2006 Pieces of Learning

Asking Smart Questions

CONNECTION QUESTIONS

DESCRIPTION Connection questions are used to promote understanding and gain perspective.

WORDING EXAMPLES

Given the vandalism statistics over the last five years, what recommendation will you make to the Board of Education regarding band instrument lockers?

How do you think the new dress code has affected student behavior?

PURPOSES

- ▶ to compare and/or contrast facts and ideas.
- ▶ to illustrate cause and effect.
- ▶ to relate a generalization to the supporting evidence.
- ▶ to relate a value, skill or definition to an example of its use.
- ▶ to communicate numerical relationships.

CONNECTION QUESTIONS

- ▶ often lead to application questions.
- ▶ are particularly helpful in understanding abstract ideas.

Note: Understanding a situation doesn't necessarily imply doing something about it.

🕷 BUGS and ↳ TROUBLE SHOOTING

- 🕷 'Discovering' a faulty relationship, due to lack of sufficient information or incorrect assumptions.
    - ↳ Check your assumptions.
- 🕷 Making intuitive leaps without adequately verbalizing them.
    - ↳ Start with small steps, and then use those to build up to the big idea through follow-up questions.

Asking Smart Questions

CURIOSITY QUESTIONS

DESCRIPTION Curiosity questions encourage exploration, playfulness, and looking at familiar things in unfamiliar ways.

WORDING EXAMPLES

Why do you think the author chose to end the story so abruptly?

What if the train could travel at 300 miles per mile? What then?

PURPOSES

- ▶ to stimulate creativity.
- ▶ to stimulate interest.

CURIOSITY QUESTIONS

- ▶ often contain words like '*what*,' *if*', '*how*', and '*why*'.
- ▶ can help people get out of a rut and see things from a different perspective.
- ▶ can't always be answered to the questioner's satisfaction.
- ▶ may sometimes be frustrating, but are not necessarily the 'dead-end' questions they seem to be.

🕷 BUGS and ↳ TROUBLE SHOOTING

🕷 Not asking curiosity questions, due to fear of seeming stupid or ignorant.

↳ Be brave! If you feel the need, you can hedge your bet by prefacing your question with, *'This may sound silly, but . . .'*

🕷 Not asking curiosity questions at all, due to fear of seeming trivial.

↳ Provide enough background information so that your question doesn't sound like a complete non sequitur.

🕷 Annoying someone who sees the question as irrelevant and/or foolish — or who simply isn't in the mood for thinking creatively.

↳ People might be legitimately annoyed if an "off-the-wall" question interrupts a serious discussion — carefully consider your timing.

© 2006 Pieces of Learning

Asking Smart Questions

EVALUATION QUESTIONS

DESCRIPTION Evaluation questions are used to make judgments of good or bad, right or wrong according to specified criteria.

WORDING EXAMPLES

Which music camp is better for a serious music student?

What are the relative merits of the Washington Post compared to the Wall Street Journal?

PURPOSES
- ▶ to identify and challenge assumptions underlying thoughts and actions.
- ▶ to reach consensus on questions of good/bad or right/wrong.
- ▶ to prompt reflective analysis, rather than to generate specific answers.
- ▶ to identify and/or compare advantages and disadvantages.

EVALUATION QUESTIONS
- ▶ are based on previously agreed upon criteria.
- ▶ include judgment/comparison words such as *better/best, worse/worst, right/wrong, good/bad, fair/unfair, reasonable/unreasonable,* etc.
- ▶ can be intimidating.
- ▶ when negative, is perceived as "criticism," when positive, is considered "constructive," or even interpreted as "praise."

BUGS and TROUBLE SHOOTING
- Creating defensive responses.
  - Focus on a possible solution, rather than on the problem.
- Creating defensive responses by failing to reach prior agreement on definition of standards.
  - Standards must be agreed on before you ask an Evaluative Question.
- Inviting evasive responses by asking questions, which are too general.
  - Limit the scope of your question.

EXPLORATION QUESTIONS

DESCRIPTION Exploration questions are designed to seek further information.

WORDING EXAMPLES

What would happen if we were to offer a high school class on comparative religions?

What can we do to prevent this sort of disaster in the future?

PURPOSES

- ▶ **to assess boundaries.**
- ▶ **to examine all aspects of the subject.**
- ▶ **to build connections among ideas and/or feelings.**

EXPLORATION QUESTIONS

- ▶ are a bit like throwing your line into the water: you never know what you might catch.
- ▶ can be used to facilitate brainstorming.
- ▶ are concerned with going beyond conventional and/or traditional responses.
- ▶ can be used to build and/or strengthen relationships.

🕷 BUGS and ↳ TROUBLE SHOOTING

🕷 Phrasing the question so that it seems to require a logical, rather than creative or imaginative, response.

↳ Make it clear you are seeking alternatives.

🕷 Asking a "what if" question and then not accepting creative or "far out" responses.

↳ Don't ask exploration questions if you don't want to explore.

Asking Smart Questions

FACT QUESTIONS

DESCRIPTION Fact questions seek specific information and require straightforward, verifiable answers.

WORDING EXAMPLES

What concrete evidence do we have?

Where will the new school bus routes go?

PURPOSE

▶ **to seek information without reference to beliefs or attitudes.**

FACT QUESTIONS

▶ often begin with who, what, when, where, and how much or how many.

▶ focus on a specific state of affairs, actual events, names, dates, or numbers.

▶ require a straight 'information answer', with no interpretation or analysis added.

▶ can be effectively used to narrow the scope of the topic.

🕷 BUGS and ↪ TROUBLE SHOOTING

🕷 Using "button-pushing" words that elicit a defensive, or emotional response.

↪ Use neutral, "just the facts, Mam" wording.

🕷 Asking questions based on beliefs and values (sometimes disguised as facts).

↪ Think like a reporter; frame your questions as objectively as possible.

🕷 Basing questions on "facts" which aren't universally accepted as factual.

↪ Check your assumptions. (essential if you are discussing a controversial issue).

🕷 Asking questions which don't necessarily have a factual answer.

↪ Stick to verifiable facts if you expect a factual answer.

Asking Smart Questions

HYPOTHETICAL QUESTIONS

DESCRIPTION Hypothetical questions ask you to *imagine* a particular situation or outcome.

WORDING EXAMPLES

What if we cancelled Spring Break and let students out earlier in the summer?

How would you feel if . . ?

PURPOSES

- ▶ to elicit answers which call for creativity within the realm of possibilities.
- ▶ to consider "what if" situations.
- ▶ to encourage expansion of ideas, opinions, and feelings.

HYPOTHETICAL QUESTIONS

- ▶ are often put in the framework of a theoretical situation.
- ▶ are helpful in determining basic attitudes or approaches.
- ▶ are useful in exploring new directions.
- ▶ are not necessarily meant to be answered.

🕷 BUGS and ↪ TROUBLE SHOOTING

🕷 Encouraging impossible, or unlikely answers.

↪ Don't ask hypothetical questions if you're looking exclusively for practical answers.

🕷 Annoying someone who sees the question as too far out.

↪ Consider your timing — people might be legitimately annoyed if a hypothetical question interrupts a practical discussion.

Asking Smart Questions

LIMITED CHOICE QUESTIONS

DESCRIPTION Limited Choice Questions include a small number of answer choices as part of the question.

WORDING EXAMPLES

Would you rather have the test in class tomorrow or as a take-home exam over the weekend?

Do you support or oppose an 'open campus' for lunch hour?

PURPOSES

- ▶ **to offer a measure of participation in the decision making process.**
- ▶ **to limit the scope of possible answers.**

LIMITED CHOICE QUESTIONS

- ▶ are unique in that the desired answer is part of the question.
- ▶ must be phrased in neutral terms.
- ▶ are dangerously closely related to hostile Double-Barreled Questions.

🕷 BUGS and ↳ TROUBLE SHOOTING

🕷 Not making the choices clear.
  ↳ Be specific.

🕷 Giving too many choices.
  ↳ Offer no more than three choices.

🕷 Unduly influencing the choice (this easily becomes a Double-Barreled Question).
  ↳ Be careful to be neutral.

MEMORY QUESTIONS

DESCRIPTION Memory Questions are used to remember what you know or have experienced.

WORDING EXAMPLES

What was happening in the story when we stopped reading yesterday?

What is the mathematical symbol for the number 3.14?

PURPOSES

- ▶ to recall previously acquired information.
- ▶ to recall feelings, experiences, and values.
- ▶ to recall how to perform a set of practiced physical skills.

MEMORY QUESTIONS

- ▶ often begin with one of the 5 *W*'s: *Who, What, When, Where,* or *Why*.
- ▶ ask for rote recall.
- ▶ tend to require a specific "right" answer.
- ▶ are sometimes inappropriately disparaged as dealing with "lower-level" thinking skills.

Note: Factual information serves as the foundation for all of the "higher-level" thinking processes, so memory is a vitally important skill to develop.

🕷 BUGS and ↳ TROUBLE SHOOTING

🕷 Focusing on knowledge, which may be regarded as trivial.

↳ If you need to know a "picky detail", it's helpful to provide memory aids.

🕷 Asking a Memory Question of someone whose memory is likely to be biased.

↳ If you're looking for straightforward answers, choose someone who doesn't have a vested interest.

Asking Smart Questions

OPEN-ENDED QUESTIONS

DESCRIPTION Open-ended questions are broad in scope, requiring thoughtful answers.

WORDING EXAMPLES

What are some ways, besides a test, that you could show what you've learned this semester?

How can studying a foreign language help you in the future?

PURPOSES

- ▶ **to elicit a wide range of answers.**
- ▶ **to ask for explanations, reasons, details, and elaborations.**
- ▶ **to request personal opinions, beliefs, values, or feelings.**
- ▶ **to explore complex issues.**

OPEN-ENDED QUESTIONS

- ▶ often begin with '*why,*' '*how,*' or '*will you tell me about,*' but, like closed questions, can begin with '*what,*' or '*do.*'
- ▶ put you in control because you direct the topics to be discussed.
- ▶ allow you:
  - ★ to foster a relaxed atmosphere.
  - ★ to leave room for the conversation to branch.

🕷 BUGS and ↪ TROUBLE SHOOTING

- 🕷 Asking questions which are so open-ended that they can't be answered with any degree of comfort.
  - ↪ Narrow your question sufficiently so it can be answered in a reasonable amount of time.
- 🕷 Asking an open question when what you really want is specific information.
  - ↪ Ask specific follow-up questions.

POLICY QUESTIONS

DESCRIPTION Policy questions seek to define a definite course of action or a procedure and are often used to establish the guidelines for outlining a specific strategy.

WORDING EXAMPLES

Should the Student Council be involved in the decision-making process at this point?

Should we allow students to do door-to-door fundraising for school projects?

PURPOSES

- ▶ to examine issues of precedence in order to determine a policy position.
- ▶ to judge whether a future action should be taken.

POLICY QUESTIONS

- ▶ usually include some form of the verb *should*.
- ▶ often offers an answer as part of the question.

🕷 BUGS and ↳ TROUBLE SHOOTING

🕷 Confusing value and policy questions; substituting one for the other.

↳ Policies are based on values. Determine which you wish to question, then stick to the appropriate format!

🕷 Phrasing the question in such a general way that it could be mistaken for a Hypothetical Question, rather than a *Policy Question* requiring a reality-based answer.

↳ Focus on things that people can do something about, rather than generalized global ideals like "democracy" or "justice."

Asking Smart Questions

PROBING QUESTIONS

DESCRIPTION Probing questions pull out and pursue thoughts, feelings, or ideas.

WORDING EXAMPLES

Exactly why do you think we need a career center?

What influenced you to become a jazz trombonist?

PURPOSES

- ▶ to thoroughly investigate a concept or a previous answer.
- ▶ to request additional details.

PROBING QUESTIONS

- ▶ are second (or third or fourth) questions, seldom first.
- ▶ can demonstrate empathy and interest, BUT
- ▶ must be asked at an appropriate time. If you ask probing questions too soon or too often in a conversation, they may come across as prying.
- ▶ should be used sparingly to avoid giving the impression that you're conducting an inquisition.

🕷 BUGS and ↳ TROUBLE SHOOTING

🕷 Asking too broad a question.

  ↳ Act like Sherlock Holmes: phrase your question to encourage in-depth information.

🕷 Failing to give sufficient time and opportunity to respond.

  ↳ Be patient — probing questions require thoughtful answers; thoughtful answers require some time.

RHETORICAL QUESTIONS

DESCRIPTION Rhetorical questions are used when no real answer is expected or even desired.

WORDING EXAMPLES

Do you think I enjoy getting terrible reports like this from the substitute?

Note: We have not included any examples of this category other than this one related to student behavior, because they would not make sense without the full explanation that follows a Rhetorical Question.

PURPOSES

- ▶ to stimulate thought about a question.
- ▶ to encourage listeners to respond internally.
- ▶ to lead the listener in a particular direction.

RHETORICAL QUESTIONS

- ▶ activate alertness in listeners
- ▶ often contain their own answers.
- ▶ can be useful to set the scene for further amplification.

🕷 BUGS and ↪ TROUBLE SHOOTING

🕷 There are no Rhetorical Question bugs unless you want a verbal answer. In that case, a Rhetorical Question would be non-productive, and you should choose a question type more appropriate to your purpose.

Asking Smart Questions

SYNTHESIS QUESTIONS

DESCRIPTION Synthesis questions facilitate the process of combining a variety of facts, ideas, and concepts into a new whole.

WORDING EXAMPLES

How can we combine Carol and Jody's ideas to create a curriculum that works for both the Nature Center staff and the school district?

We've got cottage cheese, milk, eggs, and blueberry jam left over from the Foods Class's Parent Breakfast — what kind of new dessert could we create?

PURPOSES

- ▶ to perceive the relationships among ideas and concepts.
- ▶ to shape unrelated ideas into new concepts and generalizations.

SYNTHESIS QUESTIONS

- ▶ stimulate divergent thinking and expression.
- ▶ use the "inductive reasoning" process, moving from simple elements of thought to a complex whole.
- ▶ are the opposite of analysis questions.
- ▶ do not have absolute right or wrong answers.

🕷 BUGS and ↳ TROUBLE SHOOTING

🕷 Having in mind a definite answer.

↳ Synthesis questions are, by nature, creativity-stimulants. If you are looking for a specific response, choose a different question type.

🕷 Asking insignificant questions.

↳ Synthesis questions require more time and thought than many other types. If there is no real need, don't ask.

TRANSLATION QUESTIONS

DESCRIPTION Translation questions are used to convert information from one form to another.

WORDING EXAMPLES

Would you give us a quick summary of what we've learned so far — or at least highlight the main points?

Would a pie chart showing how you use your after-school time illustrate your point about having too much homework?

PURPOSES

- ▶ to convert the spoken word into a different symbolic form: a graph, model picture, chart, numerical equivalents, music, dance, etc.
- ▶ to change technical language into layman's language.
- ▶ to condense a detailed report into a brief summary or outline.

TRANSLATION QUESTIONS

- ▶ can help enhance meaning, particularly in situations where the content of the message is complicated, or where people have unequal verbal skills.
- ▶ allow people to use visual or kinesthetic skills to communicate a message.
- ▶ serve as a check on understanding.

🕷 BUGS and ↳ TROUBLE SHOOTING

- 🕷 Making the assumption that everyone understands jargon.
    - ↳ Make sure your jargon is clearly understood if you want a usable answer.
- 🕷 Not being aware of the need for translation.
    - ↳ Check your assumptions. You may need to supply "Chapter Zero" (See INFO SITE: Question Attributes).

Asking Smart Questions

VALUE QUESTIONS

DESCRIPTION Value questions seek clarification of basic beliefs. They address issues such as the worth, excellence, usefulness or importance of a subject.

WORDING EXAMPLES

Do you believe it's appropriate for teachers to strike?

Do you think the bond issue is important enough to merit the time and energy we're devoting to it?

PURPOSES

- ▶ to determine the relative goodness or badness of what is being questioned.
- ▶ to seek responses which reveal a personal bias, preference, judgment, or opinion based on individual values.

VALUE QUESTIONS

- ▶ usually include evaluative words.
- ▶ seek advice (with or without intent to follow it).

> **Note:** This kind of question can get you into trouble if you aren't careful. When judgments and opinions are sought, many people expect their advice to be followed. Therefore, it is important to be clear AT THE OUTSET about the intention behind the question.

🕷 BUGS and ↪ TROUBLE SHOOTING

🕷 Not clearly stating the purpose of asking the question (especially dangerous if you do not necessarily intend to follow whatever advice you may receive).

↪ Make an up-front statement about how you plan to use the advice, opinion, or information you receive.

🕷 Fostering defensiveness and arguments due to conflicting values.

↪ Acknowledge the conflict, and then move on.

Asking Smart Questions

VERIFICATION QUESTIONS

DESCRIPTION Verification questions are used to double-check understanding of both spoken and unspoken messages.

WORDING EXAMPLES

You consider a year-round schedule the best way to reduce over-crowding in our schools?

You're confident you've thoroughly explored all the possibilities and haven't missed any information?

PURPOSES

- ▶ to confirm that a message has been accurately understood.
- ▶ to check whether or not expectations have been met.
- ▶ to confirm the relevance of a former statement or answer.

VERIFICATION QUESTIONS

- ▶ are useful for testing ideas.
- ▶ are effective tools in goal setting or analysis.
- ▶ when presented as a paraphrase in the form of a question, serve as a low-key, non-threatening way of encouraging elaboration.
- ▶ can be particularly practical in formal or uncomfortable situations.

🕷 BUGS and ↳ TROUBLE SHOOTING

🕷 Appearing dumb because you ask for verification.

↳ Do it anyway. Getting verification is often an important step.

🕷 Causing impatience because of the redundancy of verification.

↳ Don't ask for verification merely as a matter of course.

© 2006 Pieces of Learning

Asking Smart Questions

 **INFO SITE**

 Dictionary of Non-Productive Questions

CONFIRMING QUESTIONS

DESCRIPTION Confirming questions are used to request endorsement, ratification, sanction, or support.

WORDING EXAMPLES

Do you think this cheerleader outfit makes me look fat?

Do you agree that Joe is the best candidate for class president?

PURPOSES

- ▶ to seek agreement.
- ▶ to seek reinforcement or proof of ideas and opinions.
- ▶ to seek acceptance of ideas, opinions, values, beliefs, or even self.

CONFIRMING QUESTIONS

- ▶ can help build bridges to better understanding if they are sensitively phrased and sincerely meant.
- ▶ should not be asked unless you really want to hear the answer.

BUGS and TROUBLE SHOOTING

- 🕷 Sounding insincere.
    - ↳ Find something about which you can sincerely frame a question.
- 🕷 Agreeing at surface level only (in order to get the other person to shut up and listen to YOUR idea).
    - ↳ Show respect. Don't prematurely switch the conversation to deal with your ideas.
- 🕷 Disguising a hint as a question.
    - ↳ Be direct; ask for an opinion, not agreement.

DOUBLE-BARRELED QUESTIONS

DESCRIPTION Double-barreled questions link two separate questions as though they are one. They're evidence of fuzzy thinking.

WORDING EXAMPLES

Should we cut the school library budget; or make sure all students have a public library card?

Would it make sense to get rid of the vending machines; or should we allow an open campus at lunchtime?

PURPOSES

- ▶ *Unintentional*: are purposeless.
- ▶ *Intentional*: are intended to influence the answer by offering a semblance of choice, with the 'correct' answer made painfully obvious.

DOUBLE BARRELED QUESTION

- ▶ are often presented in an either/or format.

When used intentionally, they:
- ▶ are designed to mislead.
- ▶ may be based on second-hand opinions or attitudes.
- ▶ are confusing.
- ▶ are hard to answer because the two halves must be answered separately.
- ▶ are a set-up.

🕷 BUGS and ↳ TROUBLE SHOOTING

🕷 This Question-type is a BUG.

↳ TROUBLE SHOOTING: Don't use it!

Asking Smart Questions

DUMB-SMART QUESTIONS

DESCRIPTION Dumb-Smart questions are used to camouflage true intent.

WORDING EXAMPLES

This may sound crazy, but what if we cut the football team completely out of the school district budget?

You wouldn't have to worry about who to ask to the senior prom if we didn't have a senior prom, would you?

PURPOSES

- to provide an easy 'out' if you're wrong.
- to take the devil's advocate position in order to anticipate and counter potential negative effects.
- to help you ask a question or make a possibly hostile or demanding-sounding comment in a non-threatening way.
- to reduce antagonism toward the 'always right' person.
- to seek reinforcement or proof of ideas and opinions.

DUMB/SMART QUESTIONS

- can be used to clarify thinking about possible ramifications of a situation.
- are used when you'd prefer sounding 'dumb' to being wrong.
- can be useful, but aren't straightforward.

BUGS and TROUBLE SHOOTING

- Sounding like you're either joking or indeed, dumb.
    - Unless you're simply striving to provide a little comic relief, frame your question in such a way that your listeners have a chance of recognizing it as a serious question instead of just a joke.
- Sounding more like an obstructionist than a problem solver.
    - Don't overuse Dumb-Smart questions.

Asking Smart Questions

IMPLIED QUESTIONS

DESCRIPTION Implied questions are bona fide questions that are expected to be answered, but they're not voiced. Instead, they're buried behind or within a statement or another question.

WORDING EXAMPLES

Looking at Bill's and Mark's grades, I wonder how long it would take them to get themselves totally lost in Madrid . . .
<u>Implied Question</u>: *Do you think Bill and Mark speak Spanish well enough to profit from the exchange student program in Spain?*

Seven of you went to that meeting this morning; why can't anyone explain what was said?
<u>Implied Question</u>: *Were any of you paying attention?*

PURPOSE

▶ **to get a response without actually asking a question.**

IMPLIED QUESTIONS

▶ are passive-aggressive.
▶ may be conveyed in a gesture (raising of an eyebrow, etc.).
▶ may be disguised as a joke.
▶ seem manipulative, sarcastic, and/or devious.
▶ are often ignored because they aren't taken seriously.
▶ create defensiveness.

🕷 BUGS and ↳ TROUBLE SHOOTING

🕷 This Question-type is a BUG.
　　↳ TROUBLE SHOOTING: Don't use it!

© 2006 Pieces of Learning

Asking Smart Questions

INDIRECT QUESTIONS

DESCRIPTION Indirect questions are used to approach a topic in a roundabout manner.

WORDING EXAMPLES

I wonder why normal operating procedures weren't followed?

Isn't it odd no one seems concerned about air conditioning the building even when the heat prevents students from concentrating the last two months of school?

PURPOSES

- ▶ to 'beat around the bush' rather than tackle an issue head on.
- ▶ to facilitate discussion about a sensitive, potentially embarrassing, or threatening subject.
- ▶ to direct attention to a situation in a non-threatening manner.

INDIRECT QUESTIONS

- ▶ are less blunt than direct questions.
- ▶ can help create a positive climate

🕷 BUGS and ↳ TROUBLE SHOOTING

- 🕷 Appearing weak or wish-washy.
- 🕷 Sounding dishonest, devious, and attacking.
- 🕷 Increasing a threat instead of reducing it.
- 🕷 Being interpreted as criticism.
- 🕷 Disguising advice as a question.
    - ↳ Ask a straightforward question to trouble shoot all these BUGS.

Asking Smart Questions

LEADING QUESTIONS

DESCRIPTION Leading questions tell others what to think.

WORDING EXAMPLES

Don't you think he is doing a good job?

You understand that when you're tardy, you miss important information, don't you? And you know it delays the entire class when I have to explain things again just for you? And we've discussed the school policy about tardies, haven't we? So, what are you going to do to improve your attendance record?

PURPOSE

▶ to prod toward the answer desired.

LEADING QUESTIONS

▶ imply that agreement with the question's bias is expected.

▶ often come in strings of several questions at a time.

▶ can sometimes be effective in helping young people make good decisions.

▶ close down communication.

▶ preclude your learning anything new.

🕷 BUGS and ↳ TROUBLE SHOOTING

🕷 This Question-type is a BUG. It's fundamentally dishonest, demanding a positive response.

↳ TROUBLE SHOOTING: Don't use it!

Exception: Sometimes, working with young children or teenagers, it's more effective to use leading questions than to be 100% directive.

© 2006 Pieces of Learning

Asking Smart Questions

MESSAGE QUESTIONS

DESCRIPTION Message Questions are seldom used for seeking information. Primarily, they serve as an excuse for delivering a lecture.

WORDING EXAMPLES

Don't you think . . ? (followed by what you should think, and why).

Doesn't your textbook tell you that . . . (followed by a statement of opinion or fact, and perhaps a brief question).

PURPOSES

- ▶ to state an opinion or make a point.
- ▶ to give additional information, or just show off.

MESSAGE QUESTIONS

- ▶ sometimes sound as if they are serious questions that are meant to be answered. (But just try to break in to the speaker's monologue to do so!)
- ▶ are sometimes used as a thinly veiled attack.

🕷 BUGS and ↳ TROUBLE SHOOTING

🕷 This Question-type is a BUG. It's fundamentally dishonest and makes you sound like a bore.

↳ TROUBLE SHOOTING: Don't use it!

Asking Smart Questions

PROJECTION QUESTIONS

DESCRIPTION Projection questions are used to attribute your own feelings, opinions, and attitudes (negative or positive) to another person.

WORDING EXAMPLES

Don't you just hate (love) it when . . ?

Isn't it exciting (disgusting) that Fred finally admitted he's dyeing his hair?

PURPOSES

- ▶ to get another person to agree with you.
- ▶ to establish that you and the other person are allies.
- ▶ to reduce the effect of threatening questions.
- ▶ to determine indirectly what someone else thinks.

PROJECTION QUESTIONS

- ▶ have hidden agendas.
- ▶ can increase threat.
- ▶ are often negative in character
- ▶ can be positive when used to place yourself in another person's shoes.

🕷 BUGS and ↪ TROUBLE SHOOTING

🕷 This Question-type is a BUG. It makes you look like you're blaming others for your own shortcomings, and often creates defensive responses.

↪ TROUBLE SHOOTING: Don't use it!

Exception: It can be used — carefully and consciously — to express empathy.

Asking Smart Questions

 **INFO SITE**

 Dictionary of X-Rated Questions

(Open With Caution!)

ANTAGONISTIC QUESTIONS

DESCRIPTION Any question, asked with hostile intent, can morph into an Antagonistic question

WORDING EXAMPLES

What on earth do you mean by that nonsense?

Why didn't you listen the first six times I answered that question?

PURPOSES

- ▶ to deliberately cause discord
- ▶ to express angry disagreement.
- ▶ to mask ignorance.
- ▶ to cover up poor listening habits.
- ▶ to seek group recognition (ego enhancement).
- ▶ to cause someone to lose face, feel unimportant or uninformed.
- ▶ to delay action on a point up for decision.

ANTAGONISTIC QUESTIONS

- ▶ are used to put someone in a defensive position.
- ▶ frequently create so much dissension that they are never actually answered.

🕷 BUGS and ↳ TROUBLE SHOOTING

🕷 X-Rated Questions are, by definition, BUGS.
  ↳ TROUBLE SHOOTING: Don't use them!

BLACK HOLE QUESTIONS

DESCRIPTION Black Hole questions are dead-ends.

WORDING EXAMPLES

Who do you think you are, talking to the principal like that?

How do you expect me to act when you're so illogical?

PURPOSES

- ▶ to vent anger
- ▶ to create dissension or hurt feelings

BLACK HOLE QUESTIONS

- ▶ irritate and frustrate.
- ▶ bewilder, disconcert and perplex.
- ▶ lead to disasters (particularly in relationships).
- ▶ make you look stupid.
- ▶ stunned silence

🕷 BUGS and ↳TROUBLE SHOOTING

🕷 X-Rated Questions are, by definition, BUGS.

↳ TROUBLE SHOOTING: Don't use them!

Asking Smart Questions

GOTCHA QUESTIONS

DESCRIPTION Gotcha questions are used to discredit an idea or to mount a personal attack.

WORDING EXAMPLES

How can you be so incredibly stupid?

When are you planning to join the 21st Century — in the year 2025?

PURPOSE

- ▶ **to silence others.**
- ▶ **to put people down.**
- ▶ **to put someone on the defensive.**

GOTCHA QUESTIONS

- ▶ are used to embarrass.
- ▶ are perceived as vicious when asked by someone higher in a hierarchy.
- ▶ have the effect of silencing not only the intended victim, but just about everyone else in the vicinity as well.
- ▶ are not meant to be answered.
- ▶ are mean and nasty.

🕷 BUGS and ↳TROUBLE SHOOTING

🕷 X-Rated Questions are, by definition, **BUGS**.

↳ TROUBLE SHOOTING: Don't use them!

LOADED QUESTIONS

DESCRIPTION Loaded questions are a hostile way of pushing another person into agreeing with you.

WORDING EXAMPLES

Don't you think it's high time you showed some responsibility and stopped whining about how it's not your fault?

Wouldn't you say that hiring a retired general will guarantee the new superintendent will be behind the times and authoritarian?

PURPOSES

- **to put another person on the defensive.**
- **to deliver a (not very) veiled threat.**

LOADED QUESTIONS

- tend to have ONE implied (evident) answer.
- tend to put people into corners.
- often include phrases such as *Don't you think . . , Don't you agree that . . .* or *Wouldn't you say . . .*
- close down communication.
- may create so much hostility you find yourself being sued for discrimination or harassment.
- may virtually guarantee an untruthful answer.

BUGS and TROUBLE SHOOTING

X-Rated Questions are, by definition, **BUGS**.

⤷ TROUBLE SHOOTING: Don't use them!

HOME PAGE

The Other Side of Question Asking

...that is a very good question. I don't know the answer.
— Arthur Miller

The other side of question asking resides in the *After Zone* and has to do with answers.

How will you know a good answer when you hear it?

This may sound like the silliest of Dumb-Smart questions, but it's for real — you don't always get the precise answer you expect, and sometimes you don't even know what to expect.

What's the difference between a surprising (or perhaps even alarming) answer and a poor one?

According to Toastmasters International, good answers have several distinctive characteristics. They

▶ **are stated** *positively.*

▶ **are expressed in terms the** *listeners can understand.*

▶ **don't include** *loaded or slanted words* **(even if such words are used by the questioner as bait to set the listener up). They don't sound** *antagonistic,* *evasive* **or** *defensive.*

▶ **tend to be** *specific* **and** *concise.* **They don't include more information than necessary, but they do capitalize on opportunities in the question to offer the answerer's viewpoint.**

Asking Smart Questions

The characteristics of good answers sound a lot like the requirements for good questions, don't they? Knowing what you know about question asking, you will — like the bear who went over the mountain — be in familiar territory when you get there.

Some questions don't require an answer because they're not true questions. However, a reply is usually expected. If such a question is asked, a useful strategy is to respond with a question:

> ▶ *How do you feel about that?*
> ▶ *Are you saying . . ?*
> ▶ *Do you mean . . ?*

A good questioner should also be a good answerer. In fact, it makes sense to put the same kind of effort into answering questions as you put into asking them.

HOT TIP

What goes around comes around:

Direct and complete replies to the questions of others

Beget direct and complete replies to your next questions.

To learn more about the other side of question asking —

> **Mental Bungee JUMP**
> To
> **INFO SITE:**
> Re-phrasing Poor Questions
> Page 133

© 2006 Pieces of Learning

Asking Smart Questions

 **INFO SITE**

Listening in the Time Zones

I can never tell you what you said, but only what I heard.
— John Powell

LISTEN TO THIS:

The average person spends about 45% of each day listening!

Multiply that percent by the number of years you've been alive. What portion of your life have *you* devoted to listening? Pretty hefty amount of time!

AND LISTEN TO THIS:

Failure to listen *effectively* results in up to an 80% distortion of ideas.

Everybody knows that listening proficiency is critical to the questioning process — both asking good questions and receiving good answers depend on it. NOT everybody knows that careful listening must occur —

▶ *before* asking a question

   ▶ *while (during)* you are asking a question,

      ▶ *after* you have asked a question (to fully understand the answer),

         ▶ and to be sure you don't wander into the *seldom-if-ever* zone.

HOT TIP

LISTENING and **HEARING** are different processes.
You *hear* with your *ears*.
You *listen* with your *mind and your heart*.
(There's a profound difference!)

Asking Smart Questions

ACTIVE listening habits are the key to achieving good questioning techniques. Otherwise, your first question may be fine, but any subsequent questions may be off the mark. Active listeners, as opposed to passive listeners, act on the understanding that communication is a two-way process in which both listener and speaker bear fifty percent responsibility.

> **Note**: Active listening — which *should* occur in all the Question Zones — is especially useful in two difficult types of situations: when you're not certain what the other person means, and when you receive an important or emotionally charged message.

How NOT to Do It

Being Passive

Passive listeners tend to take in whatever is said without engaging much of their mind.

Parroting

If your first question was not accurately understood, be careful not to simply repeat it (louder and more emphatically). (This qualifies as Passive — and wimpy — Active Listening.)

Ignoring or Downplaying Feelings

If you're the kind of person who is uncomfortable when there's a strong emotional tone in a conversation, you may be tempted to ignore or try to minimize the emotional content.

Don't.

HOT TIP

You can improve your listening skills by avoiding some common listening mistakes — and by becoming an active listener.

Asking Smart Questions

ACTIVE LISTENING in the *BEFORE ZONE*

> Note: If you haven't yet bungee jumped to the
> *Before* Zone, now would be a good time!

If you've already visited the *Before* Zone, you'll recall there's a lot going on there. Most importantly, it's the time zone in which you choose an appropriate question-type.

But BEFORE that —

When you're ready to ask a question, stop and consider whether you've listened effectively to what has gone before. Even if your opening words in a conversation are a question, something has occurred before anyone speaks.

Then, you need to listen to yourself. (*'Curiouser and curiouser,'* cried Alice in *Alice's Adventures in Wonderland.*) It's easy to let words flow with little thought or planning. However, if you listen to yourself, you can adjust to the situation before you speak. Or, if the words do just pop out, you can modify and correct them. Then you're less likely to be totally surprised at the response you get.

ACTIVE LISTENING IN THE *INTERFACE* **BETWEEN THE**
BEFORE **AND** *DURING* **ZONES**

Remember this dangerous intersection? This is where you compare and contrast messages and meta-messages. Listening here can make the difference between success and crash-and-burn.

HOT TIP
Listening is the key
to deciphering meta-messages.

> Note: If you haven't yet bungee jumped to the
> Info Site: Messages and Meta-Messages,
> now would be a good time!

Asking Smart Questions

ACTIVE LISTENING IN THE *DURING* ZONE

Actively listen to yourself in the *During* Zone. If you're leading a formal discussion, you might have an entire list of questions pre-planned. That's common sense and good preparation. But that doesn't negate the need for active listening! And if the discussion isn't formal, with a pre-planned direction, it's even more important to listen in the *During* Zone — anything could happen, and if you are not actively listening, you wouldn't notice!

ACTIVE LISTENING IN THE *AFTER* ZONE

Listening actively in the *After* Zone is the name of the game. Actively listening to the answers to your questions tells you if you've been understood or if you should follow up with another question — and whether the next question should be of the same type, or an entirely different type.

Active listening in the *After* Zone means completely switching roles — from questioner to listener — and suspending your racing thoughts long enough to pay full attention to the reply you get.

HOW TO DO IT

- ▶ Refrain from 'second-guessing' replies.
  (That way you won't miss the intended meaning.)

- ▶ Refrain from framing your next question before the answerer is finished replying.

  (Step One: Give the speaker the chance to finish.)

ACTIVE LISTENING IN THE *SELDOM-IF-EVER* ZONE

As usual in the *Seldom-If-Ever* Zone, a word of caution is appropriate! Your instinct may be to close your mind and not listen. But careful listening will help you identify and avoid Not-Useful, Hostile, and Non-Productive questions.

© 2006 Pieces of Learning

Asking Smart Questions

QUESTIONNAIRE: ACTIVE LISTENING SKILLS

Sometimes, even if we mean to listen carefully, attention wanders and we miss what was said. How well do you listen? What kinds of listening skills do you have? What skills do you need to develop? What is your listening I.Q.? Complete the following questionnaire to assess your listening knowledge and skill level.

DO YOU . . .	MOSTLY	OFTEN	SOME-TIMES	SELDOM
1. assume you know what the speaker is going to say and so stop listening?				
2. clarify, if necessary, what you have heard by paraphrasing the message?				
3. think about what you are going to say in rebuttal while listening to the speaker?				
4. look like you are listening when you are not?				
5. listen with an open mind?				
6. realize that words don't always have the same meaning for different people?				
7. consider how others may react to your words?				
8. listen for messages that agree with your opinions while blocking messages that don't?				
9. look at the person who is speaking?				
10. pay attention to both the emotional and informational content of a message?				
11. interrupt when you have something important to say?				
12. know which words "push your buttons" and so prompt an emotional response?				
13. tune out people who use unfamiliar accents or poor grammar?				
14. concentrate on what is said even if you find it uninteresting?				
15. Are you aware that most people speak faster than they can listen and so adjust your speaking pace accordingly?				

Asking Smart Questions

 **INFO SITE**

Re-Phrasing Poor Questions

*The ability to ask the right question
is more than half the battle of finding the answer.*
— Thomas J. Watson

POOR QUESTIONS

You ask a bad question, you get a bad answer — garbage in and garbage out.

> **HOT TIP** The best defense against half-baked answers is to gather the appropriate ingredients and whip up a nutritious question.

> **Mental Bungee JUMP
> To
> Dictionary of
> Useful Questions
> Page 91**

POOR ANSWER PREVENTION

Next to asking excellent questions, the best approach to preventing poor answers is to simply

WAIT — Silently — for an answer.

In order to give a thoughtful answer, people may need to search their memories and organize their thoughts; that may take time. It isn't easy, but the ability to wait patiently and tolerate brief silences is the best poor answer prevention technique available.

How will you know a good answer when you hear it? This may sound like the silliest of Dumb-Smart questions, but it's for real. You don't always get the

Asking Smart Questions

precise answer you expect, and sometimes you don't even know what to expect. So how will you define the difference between an uncomfortable answer and a poor one?

> **HOT TIP**
> *If prevention fails, try some coping techniques.*

COPING TECHNIQUES

There are a variety of *poor answer coping techniques* you can try. Many involve asking more questions or paraphrasing the original question. Take a look at the following examples. Each helps preserve the respondent's self-esteem and, hopefully, your feelings as well.

HOW TO DO IT

▶ Ask the same question using different words.

- **POOR QUESTION:** *You want $10 for this hunk of junk?*

  Paraphrased questions: *Is your price on this bike firm?*
  Would you be willing to accept $10 for your bike?

- **POOR QUESTION:** *Why don't you think before you act?*

  Paraphrased Question: *Are you asking why I sent out that report without showing it to you first?*

- **POOR QUESTION:** *Why can't you make a decision?*

  Paraphrased Question: *Are you asking why I sent out that report without showing it to you first?*

Sometimes poor questions fail to define the terms of an answer. A reasonable response to that kind of problem would be: ***I don't quite understand what you mean by . . .*** Or you may need to probe deeper: ***Can you give me more details about (or an example of) . . .*** Or you may need to clarify — or even restate (preferably in slightly different terms) your original question: ***I understand what you're saying, but what I really need to know is . . .***

In addition to the coping techniques described above, it's smart to keep in mind that if your first question was unsatisfactorily answered, you'll probably need to try a different question-type for your follow-up attempt. Whatever you do, do not give up if you get a poor answer. There's almost always something you can try.

> **HOT TIP**
>
> *The old adage is true:*
> ***An ounce of Prevention is worth a pound of cure.***

Asking Smart Questions

Write your own Useful Questions for your content area.

Action

Analysis

Application

Clarifying

Closed

Confronting

Asking Smart Questions

Conjecture

Connection

Curiosity

Evaluation

Exploration

Fact

Asking Smart Questions

Hypothetical

Limited Choice

Memory

Open-Ended

Policy

Probing

Asking Smart Questions

Rhetorical

Synthesis

Translation

Value

Verification

BIBLIOGRAPHY

Dillon, J.. *The Practice Of Questioning,* International Series on Communication Skills, London and New York: Routledge, 1990.

_____."Student Questions and Individual Learning", *Educational Theory,* 1986. 36:333-41.

Frischknecht, J. and Capelli, G. *Maximizing Your Learning Potential: A Handbook For Lifelong Learning,* Dubuque, Iowa: Kendall-Hunt, 1995.

Harrah, D. "The logic of questions", in F. Guenthner and D. Gabbay (eds.) *Handbook Of Philosophical Logic,* vol. 2, Dordrecht: Reidel, 1995.

Jordon, James. "Socratic Teaching," *Harvard Educational Review,* 33, No. 1, Winter, pp. 97-98, 1953.

Joshi, A., 1983. "Varieties of cooperative responses in question-answer systems", in F. Kiefer (ed.) *Questions and Answers,* Dordrecht: Reidel, pp.229-40.

Kestler, J. *Questioning Techniques And Tactics,* Colorado Springs, Co.: Shepard/McGraw-Hill, 1988.

Leeds, D. *Smart Questions,* New York: McGraw-Hill, 1987.

Long, L., Paradise, L. and Long, T *Questioning: Skills For The Helping Process,* Monterey, Ca.: Brooks-Cole, 1981.

Page, Curtis W. and Selden, Charles. *"Just Right" Best Questions,* New York: Crown Publishers, 1987.

Payne, Stanley L. *The Art Of Asking Questions,* Princeton, New Jersey: Princeton University Press, 1973.

Sternberg, Robert J. "Answering Questions and Questioning Answers," *Phi Delta Kappan,* October, pp. 136-138, 1994.

Wilen, William W., ed. *Questions, Questioning Techniques, And Effective Teaching,* Washington, D.C.: National Education Association, 1987.

INDEX

A

Abelard, Peter 12
acronyms 44
action questions 91
active listening 129-132
After Zone 65, 82, 126, 131, 142
alternatives
  to asking questions 145
analysis questions 92
application questions 93, 98
assumptions 30, 35, 36, 98, 100, 102, 111
antagonistic questions 122
attitude 70, 71, 76-78

B

Bandrowski, James 5
basic six questions 55
  how 55, 57
  what 55
  when 56
  where 56
  who 55
  why 56
Before Zone 64-69, 130
Bengis, Ingrid 59
black hole questions 63, 123
Boswell, James 46
Bulwer-Lytton, Edward 88
bungee jumping 7, 29
Bynner, Witter 82

C

Capelli, Glenn 12, 87
Carroll, Lewis 30, 39, 41, 50, 61, 66, 68, 69, 76, 81, 83, 84
case in point 53, 72
clarifying questions 52, 94
climate 70, 77-79, 89, 90, 118

closed questions 14, 59, 95, 106
comments 46, 62
complaining 70, 71
concrete words 42
confirming questions 62, 114
confronting questions 52, 96
Congreve, William 77
conjecture questions 97
connection questions 98
context 31, 58
Craster, Mrs. Edward 28
criticism 70, 72, 76, 100, 118
curiosity questions 52, 99

D

declarative statements 46, 47
Dictionaries
  non-productive questions 114-121
  useful questions 91-113
  x-rated questions 122-125
Dillard, Annie 19
double-barreled questions 104, 115
dumb-smart questions 61, 62, 116, 126, 133
During Zone 65, 69, 77, 130, 131

E

Ecclesiastes 64
Einstein, Albert 12, 16, 62
emotional load 41, 70, 72, 76
evaluation questions 100
exploration questions 52, 101

F

fact questions 102
fillers 48

Asking Smart Questions

Fitzgerald, Penelope 81
From IQ to Iq 12
Iq Factor 12, 13

G

Gide, Andre 14
good questions 10, 11, 14, 16, 23, 25, 39, 46, 55, 67, 82, 127, 128
gotcha questions 63, 124

H

Halsey, Margaret 25
Hoban, Russell 39
Home Page
  Dictionaries 86
  From IQ to Iq 12
  Other side of question asking 126
  Question types 51
  Surfing through the time zones 64
how questions 55, 57
humor 47
hypothetical questions 103, 107

I

implied questions 61, 117, 125
indirect orders 73
indirect questions 118
Info Site
  About Questions 16
  After Zone 82
  Basic Six — Plus 55
  Before Zone 66
  During Zone 77
  Interface between zones 69
  Need For Skills 20
  Listening In The Time Zones 128
  Non-productive and X-rated Questions 114, 122

Question Asking Process 28
Question Attributes 30
Question Asking Alternatives 46
Useful Questions 91
  Seldom-If-Ever zone 64, 84, 128, 131
  Useful Questions 59
  Word Choice 39
  X-rated questions 122
Interface Between the *Before* Zone and the *During* Zone 69

J

Jargon 44, 111

K

Kipling, Rudyard 16, 55

L

leading questions 119
limited choice questions 104
loaded questions 125
listening
  active 129-132
  parroting 129
  passive 129

M

memory questions 105
Mental Bungee Jump 7
message questions 120
messages 69, 79
meta-messages 69
Miller, Arthur 126
misleading questions 65
Morris, Desmond 77

N

Nelson, Horatio 69
non-productive questions 114
  confirming 61, 114
  double-barreled 104, 115
  dumb-smart 61, 62, 116, 126, 133
  implied 61, 117, 125
  indirect 118
  leading 119
  message 120
  projection 61, 122
non-verbal messages 48, 70, 80

O

open-ended questions 106

P

pacing 32
paradigm shift 5
policy questions 107
politically Incorrect words 42
poor answer 133-135
  coping techniques 134-135
  prevention 133
poor questions 23, 133
Postman, Neil 16
Pound, Ezra 51
Powell, John 128
precise words 40
probing questions 108
projection questions 121

Q

Question askers 22
question attributes 30
question choice 19
question types 51, 61, 87
  closed questions 14, 59, 95, 106
  open questions 106
  non-productive 114
  useful 59
  x-rated 122

Questionnaires
  My Question Asking Skills 25
  What Do I Know? 14
  What Type of A Question Asker
    Am I? 89

R

Rapport 59, 77
research report 77, 79
repetition 48, 49
rhetorical questions 109
Richards, Edward H. 79
Roadside Billboard 86

S

Seldom-if-ever zone 64, 84, 128, 131
Sequencing 30, 33, 34
sexist words 42, 43
short sentence format 45
silence 47-49
Smarts 87
  Analytical 87
  Creative 87
  Practical 87
  Relationship 87
specific words 41
Sternberg, Robert 12
synthesis questions 92, 110

T

The Question 9
Time Zones 64, 128
Toastmasters International 126
translation questions 111
Twain, Mark 49

Asking Smart Questions

U

useful questions 59
  action 91
  analysis 92, 110
  application 93, 98
  clarifying 52, 94
  closed 14, 59, 95, 106
  confronting 52, 96
  conjecture 97
  connection 98
  curiosity 52, 99
  evaluation 100
  exploration 52, 101
  fact 102
  hypothetical 103, 107
  limited choice 104
  memory 105
  open-ended 106
  policy 107
  probing 108
  rhetorical 109
  synthesis 92, 110
  translation 111
  value 112
  verification 113

V

value questions 112
verification questions 113
vocabulary
  acronyms 44
  concrete 42
  jargon 44, 111
  sexist words 42, 43
Voltaire 12

W

Watson, Thomas 133
word choice 39
word emphasis 76, 77
Wordsworth, William 20

X

x-rated questions 122
  antagonistic 122
  black hole 63, 123
  gotcha 63, 124
  leading 119
  misleading 65

Z

Zones
  Before Zone 66
  Interface Between The *Before* Zone
    and The *During* Zone 69
  During Zone 77
  After Zone 82